Happy Father's Day Dad!!

Love,
Travis

HAPPY FATHER'S DAY, DAD!
MAYBE YOU CAN GET SOME TIPS
FROM JACK. ENJOY!

LOVE,
Blair

GOLDEN TWILIGHT

Sleeping Bear Press
310 North Main Street
P.O. Box 20
Chelsea, MI 48118
www.sleepingbearpress.com

Printed and bound in Canada.

10 9 8 7 6 5 4 3 2 1

Library of Congress Cataloging-in-Publication Data on file.
ISBN: 1-58536-044-9

JACK NICKLAUS *in his* FINAL CHAMPIONSHIP SEASON

GOLDEN

TWILIGHT

BY DAVID S. SHEDLOSKI

Sleeping Bear Press

*For Alexander and Elizabeth
and for Andrew*

I could be worse employed
Than as watcher of the void,
Whose part should be to tell
What star if any fell.
Suppose some seed-pearl sun
Should be the only one;
Yet still I must report
Some cluster one star short.

from
On Making Certain Anything Has Happened
by Robert Frost

FOREWORD

BY ARNOLD PALMER

As friends and rivals throughout the years, not to mention intense competitors, Jack Nicklaus and I have never passed up an opportunity to give each other the needle on just about every subject imaginable. So, naturally, I couldn't pass up the chance to get on him a little last year at Muirfield Village Golf Club when Jack casually mentioned that he would probably be playing in his last U.S. Open at Pebble Beach Golf Links.

He said this to Gary Player and me during an informal exhibition prior to his own Memorial Tournament, where Jack was being honored. It was a wonderful and an emotional day for Jack to be honored there in his hometown, and I knew that he had more emotional days ahead of him if, indeed, he was going to be playing in his final U.S. Open and British Open. I still remember my emotions as I walked the final fairway at Oakmont and St. Andrews, those historic places that meant so much to me. Quite honestly, there is no easy way to exit the stage of major championship golf.

But on that sunny spring day in Columbus, Ohio, I couldn't resist repeating a jab that I had given Jack on a number of previous occasions.

"You told me you were going to quit playing golf when you were 35 years old," I said to him, "but you are still playing, so don't give me that stuff."

All three of us had a good laugh, perhaps Gary and I a bit more. But I believe we also understood the turmoil that Jack was feeling.

When I gave up championship golf in 1995, it was the appropriate time. To say it was difficult is a vast understatement. When something is such a huge part of your life, when you have built your life around it—not necessarily made it your life, but when it has become such a focus—it is not an easy thing to let go.

I remember how emotional those moments were in 1994 at Oakmont and at my last PGA Championship at Southern Hills and in 1995 at St. Andrews, when I knew that the time had come to say goodbye. I thought of all the great things that had happened to me and it was just an overwhelming feeling. I said at Oakmont that I would like to go back and do it all again. I would, you know. They were happy times.

And I'm sure Jack feels the same way.

You want to go back and do it again because there is nothing like the thrill of competition in championship golf. It is demanding, heart-rending, frustrating, and exhilarating, all at the same time. There are few things in life that encompass all of that and give you that rush of excitement of making your mark on the game, as did the greats before you like Vardon, Jones, Sarazen, and Hogan. But along with the golf, win or lose, there are other facets to championship golf that are so rewarding. Most important among them is the friendships that you make along the way. That's what makes it truly special.

Of course, I grew up with the game of golf, learning it from my father. I couldn't help but think of him when I had played in my last U.S. Open. Thoughts of him and the time he spent with me on a golf course are among my most cherished memories. Likewise, Jack and his father were very close. Charlie Nicklaus introduced his son to the game and nurtured and supported him as he developed into such a great player. I hardly think this is a coincidence.

One more thing: I love and respect the game of golf and I know Jack does, too, just as much. That's how I knew all those years ago when Jack said he'd quit by the time he was 35 that he was fooling himself. Just think of all that he and the world of golf would have missed had he followed through on that prediction.

But, sadly, it does eventually have to end. The final season is the most traumatic and the most emotional, as you still want to compete and your body can't produce all the shots that your mind remembers.

This journey of Jack's last competitive year in all four majors lets you see a side of him few have ever seen. I have always worn my emotions on my sleeve. Jack always did his best to withhold his emotions from view—until now. As Jack says farewell, we are introduced to that side of him he kept to himself. Sit back, read on, and enjoy.

—Arnold Palmer

PREFACE

"Just don't expect me to cooperate."

I had told Jack Nicklaus in late December 1999 that I would be attending every tournament he entered in 2000 with the intention of writing an on-line chronicle of his year—expected to be his last playing in all four major championships. The idea had been germinating between Alex Miceli, the president and founder of *Golf.com*, and me as far back as May '99, when Nicklaus returned to competitive golf after hip replacement surgery.

Of course, I had hopes of making the most of this once-in-a-lifetime chance. I had hopes of writing a book to tell a more vivid and full tale than what would be possible writing on a daily deadline when news instincts are predominant. I made sure Nicklaus knew I was considering such an option so he would not be surprised if I could somehow pull together what at the outset seemed to me like an enormous challenge.

"It might be called something like, 'The Last Golden Season,'" I said, throwing out an idea I obviously hadn't thought through.

That's when he remarked about not cooperating. He meant with the title. "You never know if it will be my last year," he said playfully. "I might have to go back and defend somewhere."

As for the matter of my tagging along during a year that was so important to him, I could not have imagined in my wildest dreams that Jack would make himself so accessible. He could not have been more considerate and accommodating, given the immense demands on his time. In fact, that day at his home in North Palm Beach, Florida, he tried to make it sound as if I were the one who was going to be inconvenienced by it all.

"Boy," he said with a laugh, "are you going to be sick of me by the end of the year."

There was never a danger of that. Nor was there a chance of that adage about familiarity breeding contempt coming to fruition—at least in my regard toward him. I spent a year following one of the great athletes of our time—a dream opportunity, particularly for an Ohio kid. I had the privilege of associating with one of the finest persons you could ever know. Actually, two, since Barbara Nicklaus makes it a duet.

In an era when deconstructing legends, from Thomas Jefferson to Joe DiMaggio, seems all too easy, Jack Nicklaus achieved one more great feat in 2000. He grew in stature. For this author, that was the greatest discovery.

—*DSS*, March 2001

CONTENTS

INTRODUCTION

Forty summers had faded since there was a year in golf like 2000.

In the "Eternal Summer" of 1960, as it was so christened by author Curt Sampson, golf found itself at an historic crossroads with the waning excellence of a taciturn Ben Hogan juxtaposed to the power and charisma of Arnold Palmer, with young Jack Nicklaus and his genius emerging.

The porthole of a new millennium represented another guidepost in golf, with Nicklaus the common denominator. At 60, his genius had long ago pried him from the boundary of his peers. He was recognized as the finest golfer of the previous century, yet his focus was on proving himself all over again. With his failing eyes cast warily on his mortality, he sought to recapture the passing greatness that gave rise to his sporting immortality.

One more year. That's all he wanted in 2000—just one more year.

In the midst of his striving, however, Nicklaus was forced to confront the betrayal of time in the persona of a new young champion bent on eradicating the standards he had spent his lifetime erecting. The specter of Tiger Woods loomed over him and all of golf as the twenty-first century dawned.

Jack Nicklaus was mindful of his fallible role as the man in winter stretching back through the yesterdays to his springtime self—a role endlessly reprised by the human race. He even sensed a certain futility in the endeavor when he thought of what he had been and what the uncompromising ravages of the clock had done to him.

"I embarrass myself everyday in my own mind," Nicklaus found himself saying one day.

But it didn't matter. If Nicklaus had doubts about stirring the echoes of his greatness, he had no qualms about one more year of great effort. He was determined to ignore his age, his aches, and the turn of the calendar that tidily separated his domain from that of the next great champion.

If ever there lived a golfing Methuselah, the golfing aficionados figured it to be Nicklaus. As 2000 neared, pundits and peers shared a view of the Golden Bear as an athlete past his prime but still imminently dangerous. He had a new hip, old guile, and still the sharpest mind in the game. There remained merit to any hypothetical in which his name was inserted.

One more year. Was the greatness still there? It didn't matter. Seeing greatness was a certainty, regardless of the results, which was reason enough to follow Nicklaus throughout his final championship season.

Still, many people were convinced Nicklaus had an encore in him.

"I rather envy you," PGA Tour commissioner Tim Finchem told me in January before the MasterCard Championship in Hawaii, where Nicklaus was to begin his season, "because you know that Jack is going to do something special somewhere."

Finchem predicted Nicklaus would be a legitimate contender at the Masters or the U.S. Open. In a fantasy golf league, CBS golf anchor Jim Nantz picked the Bear to win the PGA Championship. To a man, old rivals like Arnold Palmer, Gary Player, Tom Watson, Lee Trevino, and Johnny Miller confided that the odds on Nicklaus were long, but that they would still be hesitant to bet against him.

As the year wore on, the enormity of the challenge confronting Nicklaus would grow exponentially with the compounding number of heroic feats by the game's undisputed new master. Tiger Woods would win three of the four majors, obliterate records, and cause to blur the definition of "great" in the minds of many. The two men, Nicklaus and Woods, somehow seemed linked long before the 2000 season, but the year would come to mark a poignant passage for them and for the game.

No less than Watson looked upon the 100th U.S. Open at Pebble Beach, where Nicklaus bowed out while all of golf history bowed to Woods, as a singular galvanizing moment.

"I think when history looks back at it, that was a monumental U.S. Open," he said.

⤵

Golf converts oddly well into words, John Updike wrote. The proof is in the immense exhaustion of both oral and written expression on the subject. What it most definitely does not do is convert well into lasting contentment. Golf being a tantalizing game of opposites, the most successful players tend to be the least contented. But it's probably this catch-22 that drives them to the summit and keeps them there. In his mammoth 2000 season Tiger Woods never seemed to lack for desire. He continually found new sources of motivation.

Which brings us back to Jack Nicklaus. When the subject is golf of a higher order we always will be brought back to Nicklaus. He is the enduring standard.

We can spend long hours talking of Nicklaus' famed powers of concentration and his intractable optimism, both of which served as wonderful complements to his physical abilities. But one inescapable truth is no man ever achieved anything without the spark of self-motivation. Nicklaus must possess divine quantities of ambition. What else could propel him to the pinnacle of the game and allow him to remain there so long?

By the same token, what force other than inner drive could propel him at age 60 to work so hard and so passionately to compete against athletes 30 and even 40 years younger?

One more year. That's all Jack Nicklaus was asking of himself.

One more year. That's all the golf world was asking of Jack Nicklaus.

Days can be long but the years are short and our heroes can slip away from us in a blink of an eye. This book was written to preserve that blink, and fulfill, as I once read, one of the most basic and enduring human needs, that of storytelling.

The year 2000 turned out to be one of the most compelling in golf history—when there occurred a collision of eras.

Forty summers had faded since the game had seen anything like it.

1
STIRRINGS
PRELUDE TO A CURTAIN CALL

Jack Nicklaus and Tiger Woods marched briskly, stride-for-stride, off the tee and down the 18th fairway at Valhalla Golf Club as a late summer sun blazed low on the horizon.

Was the sun setting or was it rising?

Dawn or twilight?

It depended on the viewpoint. It was Friday, August 18, 2000, and as the two undisputed titans of golf traversed the final hole in the second round of the 82nd PGA Championship in Louisville, Kentucky, the sun's failing altitude stretched their shadows ominously across the golfing landscape, a literal manifestation of their position in the game.

Two long shadows, stretched across the millennial boundary that so neatly served as the dividing line between their eras. Two shadows stretching toward a common goal, but heading to contrary destinations. Two shadows that intersected for the briefest of moments, here, in a major championship, the final major of 2000, the only place in the time-space continuum where souls of a common society could meet.

Nicklaus, 60 years old, regarded as the greatest golfer of the previous century, was attempting to author a suitable final chapter to a storybook career full of happy endings. Woods, chasing the Golden Bear's unparalleled record of 18 major professional championships with a zeal scarcely contained and a success scarcely believed, for more than a year had been forcing the hand of destiny to knight him the rightful heir to the kingdom Nicklaus soon would be leaving.

Dawn or twilight?

The difference is nearly imperceptible, except to the men who cast the shadows. The laws of nature dictate that in matters of earth and sky, shadows grow longer where the sun sets or where the quiet spectacle of mortality approaches culmination.

Twilight was bearing down on Jack Nicklaus with ruthless vigilance and tens of thousands of people surrounding the last hole sensed both the urgency and the possibility of the moment. For some 40 years the Golden Bear had been able to impose his iron will on the 18th hole of practically any golf course on earth. So it was that he needed to do it once more and the bulging galleries who had been cheering him unrelentingly for two days let loose with full-throated exhortations. "Jack! Jack! Jack!"

What they were asking for was not impossible. It was nothing more than what Nicklaus had asked of himself all his life: excellence. At five over par for the championship, Nicklaus had to find a way to take no more than three strokes on the par-5 18th hole. The eagle would allow him to make the 36-hole cut and play on the weekend in what could be his final appearance in one of golf's four Grand Slam tournaments.

In stark contrast, Woods was at 10 under par, tied for the lead in his quest to become the first player in 63 years to successfully defend his PGA title. There was Woods, who already had won the U.S. Open and British Open earlier in the year by 15 and eight strokes, respectively, trying to grind out one more birdie so that he could claim the outright lead, a position from which it is almost impossible for his peers to extricate him.

There was Woods sharing footsteps with Nicklaus, walking in his idol's footsteps as a newly minted career Grand Slam champion, and yet blazing his own trail with a succession of scoring records and mesmerizing margins of victory that had sent the rest of the pro golf population reeling in disbelief.

Dawn or twilight?

Fifteen shots separated the two men. Thirty-six years separated them. One hundred thirty-seven major championships separated them.

Their spirits united them.

Who but Nicklaus could fully understand the magnitude of what Woods had accomplished in his short stint on the PGA Tour and the dominating manner in which he had done it? Who but Woods could fully appreciate Nicklaus' breathtaking record and the brazen determination it had required to compile it?

Both men had eagerly anticipated this pairing, one chance to play together in competition before the porthole of time closed on them. As Nicklaus and Woods pushed on at the last hole, each man had a chance to illuminate his essence.

Nicklaus, after laying up on his second shot, was faced with a 72-yard pitch that had to go in the hole. His swing, with a sand wedge, produced more with the memory of his greatness than the exactness of his muscles, was as good as any mortal could muster. The ball landed five feet past the flagstick, took one hop and spun backward. With each revolution of the ball, the roar of the crowd increased proportionately.

Woods was standing to the right of the green after his 3-wood second shot on the 542-yard hole dove into the deep bunker in front of the large horseshoe-shaped green. From the elevated putting surface, he had just about the best vantage point to see Nicklaus' ball land on the putting surface and dance in the direction of the hole. For a few tantalizing seconds it looked to be heading nowhere but in the cup. The shadow of the ball actually disappeared in the hole, but the ball itself defied the collective will of all who were watching it, slid by on the lower left side, and came to rest 18 inches away. Woods smiled approvingly as Nicklaus made his way onto the green and slapped the old warrior's hand as the overflow congregation exploded with whoops and applause.

Then the No. 1 player in the world settled into the bunker to tackle his own task. He splashed out of the sand to 15 feet and there was no doubt about his birdie putt finding its way in. He plucked the ball smartly from the hole and stationed himself at the back right portion of the green. When Woods turned, he exchanged a glance with Nicklaus, who pointed at him, nodded, and offered a thumbs-up sign. Woods, grinning, returned a nod.

The tiny gesture abounded with class and context, for at that moment the great Golden Bear had given the young Tiger a virtual stamp of approval, acknowledging his ascendancy to that place in the golf spectrum he was the last to occupy.

Twilight had passed into dawn.

Nicklaus stepped up to his ball promptly and sank his bittersweet birdie putt. He turned left and then right to wave to the appreciative thousands, and exited without delay. He did not look back.

⌁

"I've never been a reflector. Never done that. I've enjoyed what I've done, but I look forward to tomorrow. I look forward to what I'm doing, and where I'm going. It's a lot more fun to be working towards something than just waiting for your life to end."

Seated poolside in an easy chair behind his sprawling home in North Palm Beach, Florida, Jack Nicklaus addressed a gathering of about two dozen reporters who had convened for what is known as the "State of the Bear" press conference. From 1971 to '96, Nicklaus had hosted the news conference at the beginning of the year as a way to accommodate the countless interview requests from the media.

It was a telling gesture that he agreed to reprise the news conference on December 21, 1999, at the behest of Scott Tolley, director of communications for his company, Golden Bear International. The "State of the Bear" conference traditionally consists of a review of the previous season and a look ahead to the coming year. That there was no press conference in 1997 or '98 spoke volumes about Nicklaus' assessment of the immediate past and his future prospects. It was apparent Nicklaus now deemed himself ready to compete.

Aside from his miraculous performance at the 1998 Masters, when at age 58 and playing essentially on one leg he finished tied for sixth (after trailing the leader by just two strokes at Amen Corner), there was little Nicklaus cared to discuss about those two seasons. But as the days filtered out the remnants of the twentieth century and a new millennium approached, Nicklaus had much to discuss because he had much to look forward to.

The 2000 season held more promise than any in the past eight to 10 years even as it loomed as his last at the highest levels of professional golf. It simultaneously represented a comeback and farewell season. Nicklaus, healthier than he had been in a decade after undergoing hip replacement surgery early in '99, indicated 2000 would be the final year in which he would play in all four major championships: the Masters, United States Open, British Open and PGA Championship. This was monumental considering Nicklaus had been competing in majors since he was 17 years old, had won a record 18 of them professionally, and had appeared in more consecutive majors and more overall than any player in history.

It would be retirement from the one thing he enjoyed most in golf—major championships.

The time, he figured, was right. He'd be 60 years old, an age long past when athletes in other sports are competitive. He would be playing in the centennial U.S. Open Championship in the final year of an unprecedented three-year block of special exemptions granted by the U.S. Golf Association. Most importantly, he had a personal attachment to the golf courses hosting the majors, which made them appropriate places for him to bow out—if indeed that is what he intended to do. Or, even better, perhaps they would be places where he could conjure up one last bit of magic. The stars could not have been aligned any better.

The major championship rotation consisted of a dream lineup that included three compass points in his golfing life: Augusta National Golf Club, Pebble Beach Golf Links, and the Old Course at St. Andrews. Augusta and St. Andrews he describes as his two favorite places in golf, where the aura and the setting instill in him an abiding inspiration. Pebble Beach, meanwhile, simply is his favorite golf course.

"If you would have me name three golf courses that I would want to play majors on that I thought I had my best chance on, I would name Augusta National, Pebble Beach and St. Andrews," Nicklaus said.

The journey would begin in April with his return to the Masters at Augusta National, where he had won a record six green jackets, and where he thought, because he knew the course so intimately, he could always find a way to compete, just like he did in 1998.

His next stop would be the U.S. Open at Pebble Beach Golf Links, where Nicklaus won the 1972 national title, one of his record-tying four Open victories, as well as his second U.S. Amateur title in 1961 and three Bing Crosby National Pro-Am events. The U.S. Open always had been the most important of the four majors to Nicklaus. It was the first professional major in which he competed. That was in 1957 at Inverness Club in Toledo, Ohio. A return to Pebble Beach in mid-June in the 100th Open championship represented twice the motivation, not only because it is his favorite course, but also because of the special exemption, which he expected to be his last.

The Old Course at St. Andrews, in Scotland, awaited him in July for the British Open. To Nicklaus, the Open is his favorite tournament and St. Andrews is the optimum place to play it. "St. Andrews is the most special place to win a golf tournament," said Nicklaus, who captured two of his three Open championships at the birthplace of golf. His first win on the Old Course, in 1970, was one of the more momentous of his career. Bobby Jones, idolized by Jack and his father, Charlie, long ago said no record would be complete without a win at the ancient seaside links. Charlie Nicklaus died earlier that year of cancer and an emotional Jack dedicated that win to his dad.

Finally, there was Valhalla, the PGA track where his run would end. It lacked historical aura and contemporary respect, but Nicklaus proudly embraced the 20-year-old course as his sendoff site because it was his own creation. In fact, counting senior events, four of the year's eight majors would be contested on Nicklaus designs. (And he had overseen renovations on another two, Augusta and Pebble Beach.) Closure at Valhalla fittingly melded the twin spires of his professional life.

In a sense, the modern major championships are a Nicklaus creation, too.

Arnold Palmer, while taking the game to new levels of popularity, identified today's four major events in 1960 when he captured the Masters and U.S. Open and boldly set off for Scotland, proclaiming that a win in the British Open at St. Andrews followed by victory at that year's PGA Championship at Firestone Country Club in Akron, Ohio, would give him the Grand Slam.

The notion that there was such an achievement in golf, or that it was possible, had not been recognized since the days of Jones, who in 1930 won what was then recognized as the four Grand Slam events of golf, the "impregnable quadrilateral" consisting of the open and amateur championships of the U.S. and Britain.

But whereas Palmer identified the modern Grand Slam tournaments, Nicklaus defined them.

"He personified them," said Ben Crenshaw, a two-time Masters champion and an erudite golf historian. "It was a common feeling to wonder, 'Where is he?' no matter what else was going on in the championship. You just knew he was around somewhere and you were waiting for him to make his presence felt."

The immensity of the Nicklaus legacy in the major championships reaches beyond the raw achievement of 18 victories—20 counting the two U.S. Amateur titles in 1959 and '61. No matter how you choose to sculpt the data, the results are mountainous. Nicklaus shares or holds the record for most wins in all but the British Open. He was runner-up a record 19 times and was third on nine occasions. He finished in the top five 54 times and in the top 10 on 73 occasions, underscoring the omnipresence he exacted on any given championship. The next best total, 46, belongs to Sam Snead.

He is the only player to win the U.S. Open in three different decades, and he has made 36 cuts, one of his many Open marks. During the 1970s he did not finish out of the top 10 in the Masters. At the British Open there was a remarkable 15-year stretch beginning in 1966 where he finished no worse than tied for sixth. In the PGA he placed among the top five 14 times.

Winner of 70 PGA Tour titles and 100 events worldwide, Nicklaus was truly rare in his ability to sustain his competitiveness over so many years and against waves of fresh competitors intent on knocking him off. In the 100 major championships in which he competed from 1962 to 1986, Nicklaus finished in the top three 46 times—nearly half his appearances. Fourteen times in the 16-year stretch from 1962 to '77 he placed in the top three in two of the four majors. He had eight seasons in which he was among the top three in three of the four, and twice more he missed out on that distinction with a fourth-place thrown in. His most dominant stretch was 1971-77. In 28 majors he never finished out of the top 11 and he won six times.

⌣

"Arnold brought into focus the Grand Slam. Jack brought continuity to them that gave fans an idea of what they were about," said PGA Tour commissioner Tim Finchem. "He created the whole concept of what the majors mean in the modern era. Jack ingrained it into our consciousness: 'This is what golf is all about—performing at the highest levels.' For more than 25 years golf, in one sense, has been all about Jack Nicklaus and the major championships. He jumped up on that platform and made it his career. He thrived on it."

In the process, the majors thrived on him and his aura. Each of Nicklaus' 18 major victories not only validated his abilities, but also verified the importance of the other major championships. The PGA, for example, suffers from the occasional identity crisis, but Nicklaus won it five times and it is no less a part of his legacy. In addition, his triumphs elevated the intrinsic worth of the sites on which they were realized. Pebble Beach, Muirfield, St. Andrews, Baltusrol, Firestone, Oakmont, Oak Hill, Canterbury, Augusta: none need the Nicklaus name, but each rises in historical stature by its association with him. By the same token, Nicklaus served as an undeniable barometer for others. Winning a major championship always was meaningful, but vanquishing Nicklaus provided a context that elevated the achievement. To have beaten Nicklaus was to have passed the supreme test.

Last of all, Nicklaus' sheer presence came to be an expected element of a major championship, like the wind and whins of a British Open, the narrow fairways of a U.S. Open, or the glassy, granite greens of Augusta National and the Masters. Through 1999 he had played in 155 Grand Slam tournaments, including 146 in a row as a professional, which is one of those records that defies believability, not to mention attainability. He had made 40 starts in the Masters, 43 in the U.S. Open, 36 in the PGA, and 36 in the British Open.

If Tiger Woods stays healthy he could tie that number at the 2028 Masters. To surpass the record, he will have to compete through the 2033 British Open. He would be 57 years old. So many things would have to go right for Woods to get there; his health, his hunger level, and his playing proficiency all would have to remain intact for another 32 years against waves of younger and stronger challengers. If Woods can sustain his current blistering clip of five major victories every four years, he could pass Nicklaus' 18-win benchmark sometime in 2013. Then all he would have to do is play 20 more years to better Jack's streak of 154 straight major tournaments. That's all. Could it be any more daunting?

Nicklaus' staying power is unmatched by all but a few of the all-time great athletes of any era. Kareem Abdul-Jabbar, the NBA's career scoring leader, threw down skyhooks until he was 42. Nolan Ryan, baseball's strikeout king, flung fastballs at 46. George Blanda played 26 years in the NFL as a quarterback and kicker and was 48 when he retired. Any discussion of longevity must include Lou Gehrig and Cal Ripken Jr., baseball's iron men. The most rare and remarkable athletes are those who can remain competitive well beyond what would be considered their prime years.

Nicklaus' prime stretched 24 years, from the time of his first U.S. Open victory in 1962 to his '86 Masters triumph. That is like eons in golf, a sport in which dominance is usually confined to less than a decade. The glory years of nearly all the great players of the last century, from Bobby Jones to Byron Nelson, Ben Hogan, Arnold Palmer, Billy Casper, Tom Watson, Johnny Miller, and Seve Ballesteros, lasted no more than 10 years. The exceptions: Gene Sarazen, Lee Trevino, Sam Snead, and Gary Player, with Player's 17-year span the longest.

Jack Nicklaus grudgingly surmised that he couldn't win another major championship—"the chances, honestly, are slim," he said— but he was not willing to express outright capitulation. Why would he with thoughts of '98 still fresh in his mind? Often he enjoyed reciting a playfully defiant response to the question of his retirement: "Who knows? I may have to go back and defend somewhere."

Nicklaus, however, his truthfulness unfailing, didn't pull punches when pressed seriously. "Sure I feel like I'm going to be competitive. I wouldn't waste my time otherwise. That's not how I've been throughout my career."

This wasn't mere braggadocio. In the final weeks of 1999 Nicklaus competed in a number of made-for-television events, or so-called "Silly Season" events, and came away from them encouraged after winning three of four. After falling in the opening round of the Senior Match Play Challenge, Jack was a member of the winning Senior PGA Tour team in the Wendy's Three-Tour Challenge. Next he joined his son, Gary, in a sudden death victory over Raymond and Robert Floyd at The Office Depot Father-Son Challenge and completed the cycle by teaming with Tom Watson to capture the senior portion of the Hyundai, nee Diners Club, Matches.

"It's great to see him back with that kind of enthusiasm," Watson said after watching Nicklaus shoot 62 on his own ball at Pelican Hill Golf Club in Newport Coast, California. "After (the matches) he was like a 20-year-old kid again."

"It's just neat to see Jack playing good golf," Tom Kite said after the Father-Son Challenge. "I remember watching him hit balls at Pinehurst in 1999 and he was pathetic and in such pain. What a difference. He looks athletic again. It doesn't surprise me at all. Jack Nicklaus always has done some amazing things."

Granted, all three wins came in team events, but Nicklaus struck the ball solidly, scored decently, and most importantly, he was pain-free in his left hip, which bolstered his confidence more than anything else. "I'm so excited about being physically fit. As I saw my body deteriorate over the last five or six years, I just didn't have a whole lot of fun knowing that the next year wasn't going to be as good as the last one.

"No doubt I think a lot of optimism comes from getting my hip replaced. If you are going to play you've got to be prepared. And if you can't prepare, you can't compete."

Nicklaus underwent surgery January 27, 1999, at New England Baptist Hospital in Boston. Dr. Benjamin Bierbaum, in a 90-minute procedure, replaced his left hip with a ceramic prosthesis. Nicklaus relented, he insisted, for quality of life, but Nicklaus would not be Nicklaus if there hadn't been a quality of golf issue, too.

"I feel like there are some things I still could do," he revealed just before the operation.

Nicklaus endured intermittent problems with the hip throughout his career, ever since he injured it in the 1963 Lucky International and underwent a series of cortisone shots to alleviate the pain. Nicklaus theorizes that the injections accelerated the deterioration of the joint. By 1992 he could no longer ignore the continual pain and stiffness and he even noted to his wife, Barbara, at the PGA Championship at Bellerive Golf Club in St. Louis that he was unable to complete his golf swing.

Over the next several years Nicklaus exhausted every nonsurgical remedy imaginable in an attempt to rehabilitate it and managed through rigorous stretching and exercise to maintain nominal function. But he couldn't reverse the condition. Arthritis had set in and the cartilage in the joint was gone, replaced by calcium deposits and bone spurs. Somehow, he shot a final-round 68 in the '98 Masters on one good leg and became the oldest player to post a top-10 finish at Augusta. He made the cut in the U.S. Open at Olympic Club in June, but weeks later he reached a critical point. The pain was unbearable and the leg was going numb. He skipped the British Open at Royal Birkdale and ended his renowned streak.

By the end of 1998 he was certain he could no longer play golf —he was almost totally incapacitated in fact—and that's when he agreed to have the operation.

⌐

There were other reasons to welcome the coming year. A recipient of practically every top honor in a slew of "end of century" awards that recognized him as either the greatest golfer or among the greatest athletes, Nicklaus was due to receive one of the most gratifying honors of all in May when he would be the Honoree of the 25th Memorial Tournament, the event he founded and hosts at Muirfield Village Golf Club in Dublin, Ohio. Additionally, Nicklaus was closing in on his 200th golf course design. The completion of the Nicklaus Museum, five years in the formation and a lifetime in the making, was expected by year's end. (It was later delayed until spring of 2001.)

As '99 came to a close, Nicklaus was optimistic that business problems related to his public company, Golden Bear Golf Inc., were finally clearing up, which would lift a heavy emotional burden from him.

Nicklaus called the Golden Bear Golf fiasco "one of the most traumatic experiences of my life." Though not of his own making, the collapse of the company that he took public in 1996 and its stock, listed as "JACK" on the NASDAQ exchange, was personally embarrassing and nearly ruinous financially. Shareholders filed a class action suit in 1998 after the company restated its financial results to show a $24.7 million loss instead of $2.7 million originally reported by its subsidiary, Paragon Construction Co.

Nicklaus was visiting Cabo del Sol, in Los Cabos, Mexico, when he received a fax outlining the extent of the damage at Paragon Construction Co. His pilot, Ron Hurst, delivered the message. Hurst, like many others, was stunned. He had purchased nearly 12,000 shares of Golden Bear Golf and even cashed in a life insurance policy to buy more for as much as $20 per share. Hurst avoided catastrophic financial damage, though he lost thousands of dollars. Such pain inflicted on those closest to him stung Nicklaus more than his own losses.

"That's the kind of person we're talking about," Hurst said. "He is generous and he is loyal and all he expects in return is the same loyalty. He trusts people and he ends up getting hurt and it just isn't fair."

In the course of making things right, Nicklaus paid out more than $10 million of his own money, nearly all of his net worth. Few people would know the extent of the damage, though one who did was Arnold Palmer, who privately worried about his friend's financial outlook. But as the calendar turned over, Nicklaus felt some relief in knowing much of the heartache and legal wrangling was behind him and he could concentrate on his game.

But the most intriguing and exciting development for Nicklaus was that his son, Gary, would be joining him on the PGA Tour. The fourth of Jack and Barbara's five children, Gary altered the tenor of the year when he earned his PGA Tour card in November at the PGA Tour National Qualifying Tournament.

The younger Nicklaus, 30, put on a clutch display of golf reminiscent of his father when he shot a final-round 7-under-par 63 November 22, 1999, on the Gold Course at Doral Resort and Spa in Miami, Florida. Beginning the day on the cut line, Nicklaus ended up tied for 12th among 169 competitors. The top 35 and ties earned their cards in the grueling six-day event covering 108 holes. Gary is the offspring who looks most like his father—same face, same build, same mannerisms, same smirk—who exhibited the greatest aptitude for golf, and who was the youngest to beat his dad. His 63, which gave him a 406 total, was the lowest round of the final day and followed on the heels of a final-round 68 in the second stage of qualifying at Bear Lakes Country Club in West Palm Beach, Florida, which propelled him to the final.

Competing beside his boy was a proposition Nicklaus relished and gave him incentive to want to play a more comprehensive schedule. "I want to be around to watch Gary a little, work with him, and I want him to work with me," Jack said. "There are not many fathers who are in the position I'm in and have the opportunity to compete with their son."

"His reaction (to earning a berth on the PGA Tour) was pretty neat," said Gary, a bit more of a taciturn sort than his dad. "After I got my card he got real excited to be out here to play with me, compete against me, travel with me a little and watch me in my first year."

The watching part was going to be the shakiest aspect. "I'm like every other father," Jack said. "I live and die with his joys and failures and successes. Sometimes I am a basket case. I remember when son Jackie won the North and South Amateur in 1985. We played Muirfield the next week and I was so worn out I was terrible. It's harder to watch than it is to play. Barbara calls me the worst gallery."

But he always has been a devoted spectator, keeping up a nearly untenable travel schedule to catch whatever important football, basketball, or baseball game in which his children might be involved. In that vein, Nicklaus had walked in his son's gallery for each of the first five rounds of the qualifying tournament, but other responsibilities pulled him away the final day—responsibilities incumbent upon the golfer of the century and the world's leading golf diplomat; responsibilities incumbent on a friend.

Palmer's wife, Winnie, had died a few days earlier of ovarian cancer. Her funeral was held in Latrobe, Pennsylvania, Arnold's hometown, on the Monday of the final round of Q-School. Jack and Barbara Nicklaus wanted to be there for Arnold. Jack and Arnold had gone round and round through the years, but their friendship had endured their extended bouts of competitive animosity.

Immediately after the service, Arnold, knowing how important the day was to the Nicklaus family, approached Jack and wasted no time inquiring about Gary's progress.

"I haven't had a chance to check," Nicklaus said out of respect for his friend. Palmer responded, "Well, what are you waiting for? Let's go find out."

Nicklaus borrowed a cell phone from Hurst and dialed teacher Rick Smith, Gary's swing instructor who was following along. Jack hung on the line and grew more excited with each successive birdie his son registered. By the time Gary reached the 18th hole, a long par 4 with a second shot to an island green, Arnold and Jack were like two kids rooting for the home team and hanging on every shot of the younger Nicklaus.

The kid hit a perfect drive on the last hole, and upon hearing this from Jack, Arnold switched from cheering to coaching mode.

"Tell him to lay up. Tell him to lay up," Arnold shouted.

"You never laid up in your career," Jack pointed out.

"Yeah," Palmer said without missing a beat, "maybe if I had I'd have beaten you more."

⌐

Gary's ascension to the ranks of the PGA Tour after a nine-year sojourn that took him to nearly every tour around the world was the last piece to a puzzle that for Jack Nicklaus had been coming together almost by magic. The 2000 season already promised to be special. Gary further altered the tenor of things.

"Gary got his card and Jack suddenly thought he was 25 again. He decided, 'Hey, I want to go out and beat that kid,' Barbara said. "All of a sudden everything came into focus."

Now he had to put everything together. Nicklaus believed he could because he always did it before when he worked diligently and with a singular focus. In fact, he had not worked harder on his golf game since 1980, when he retooled his swing after his first winless pro season in '79. The result: two more major titles. He worked equally hard to become more fit. Wearing T-shirts adorned with the words "Under Construction," he threw himself into a strength program under the direction of Doug Weary, a trainer in Jupiter, Florida, who had created a training regimen for Jackie. When he first visited Weary in the summer of '99, Nicklaus couldn't perform 10 leg extensions with 70 pounds. By year's end, without ever missing a day, he was doing 20 repetitions at 260 pounds followed by a dozen more at 300 pounds. He had added four inches to his chest and subtracted one from his waist.

Such progress comes at a high cost, but Nicklaus is used to paying the price. Possessing enormous self-discipline, he has been paying all of his adult life. He hasn't missed a day of exercise in the last 15 years—including the day of his hip surgery. Golf is a lonely game, and you can feel alone even in front of 50,000 people. But to reach the summit requires a disproportionate sacrifice of more lonely hours spent beating balls and building up strength in body and mind. The sacrifice was especially large for Nicklaus, a dedicated family man.

By his reckoning there was nothing preventing him from reconstituting himself into a contemporary competitor. Nothing except age, but age to him was just a number.

But was it realistic for him to think he could elevate his game in the vicinity of that produced by Woods and David Duval and Ernie Els? Never mind the PGA Tour; competing on the Senior PGA Tour was going to be daunting enough. Nicklaus had won 10 times, including eight senior majors—the only player to capture the career Grand Slam on the 50-and-over circuit—despite nothing more than a token schedule. But heading into 2000, only eight times in the history of the Senior Tour—590 events—was the winner 60 or older.

The facts indicated the odds were long. Only one figure altered the equation: the man himself.

"You always say with Nicklaus the rules do not apply," cautioned Johnny Miller, NBC-TV golf analyst and former U.S. Open and British Open champion.

"Nothing would ever surprise me about Jack Nicklaus," longtime competitor and close friend Gary Player added. "He always has a little white rabbit he can pull out of a hat."

Told of these predictions, Nicklaus smiled knowingly. "I think I have a reasonable chance at any of the four tournaments; I might just scare the kids somewhere. I'm looking forward to the season and finding out if I can play. I can't remember the last time I played when I was really healthy. That will be a big determination of how successful I can be."

Success, of course, can be a relative thing. With Nicklaus it boiled down to scraping off the rust and the dust and having the opportunity—probably one last opportunity—to conjure up some semblance of the player who once dominated golf but for some time had been trapped inside a prematurely deteriorating frame. The last six to eight years Nicklaus was forced to compromise his pride on the golf course because he wasn't physically able to play golf in the manner formulated by his nimble mind. He couldn't attack a golf course, couldn't attempt certain shots. He knew fans appreciated him just for showing up, but the thought of what he was showing them dismayed him.

"I've never wanted to go out there and have people see just a part of Jack Nicklaus," he said, echoing sentiments similar to those once expressed by the late Joe DiMaggio. Grizzled *New York Post* columnist Jimmy Cannon asked the Yankees centerfielder once late in his career why he worked so hard every day. "There might be some kid who never saw me play before," DiMaggio responded.

The 2000 season was to be about challenges, which always kept him looking ahead. Never a reflector, Nicklaus, nonetheless, did have one legitimate reason to glance back—for a blueprint.

"I'm going to have to go back into the pool…my own talent pool," he said. "The way I look at it, I'm competing against me. I'm trying to find out what I can do."

That's what he needed to know. Who was he and what could he do? In a way the 2000 season presented a classic paradox. Jack Nicklaus planned to retire at the end of the year, but the fervor with which he prepared for the coming season indicated his intent to prove he was unfit to quit.

"Does winning ever get old?" he asked aloud, exposing the base instincts that constituted his one true identity. "I'd like to find out how old it can get."

So it was that Nicklaus, emboldened by better health and inspired by his son and a sense of opportunity, set out to rediscover his golf game or whatever remnants of it remained. The year was not about sentimental journeys, saying goodbye, ceremonial appearances or intermittent displays of his once-great skills. It was about him and his golf game.

It was about his life.

2
SUNRISE
THE JOURNEY BEGINS

The diluted strains of a ukulele cued a gathering of some 200 well-wishers surrounding the 10th tee at Hualalai Golf Club to burst into a stilted but sincere rendition of "Happy Birthday." The recipient of the serenade had just stepped onto the tee box to begin his first tournament of the millennium. Taken by surprise, Jack Nicklaus straightened up and then bowed slowly in appreciation as colored balloons billowed in the breeze. The brilliant Hawaiian sunshine hinted at promise.

It was Friday, January 21.

New dawn. New day.

Old man, but new man.

On his 60th birthday Jack Nicklaus was starting all over.

New century. The last one belonged to him. How many men could say that? How many men could look over their shoulder and watch the power of their legacy continue to grow? How many men could do that and yet choose not to do it? Look back? For what? Accommodating nostalgia is the last thing for which Jack Nicklaus would make time.

He was in Hawaii, on the Big Island, to begin another season, his 39th as a professional golfer. He was on a course he designed for the MasterCard Championship, the season-opening event on the Senior PGA Tour. He was there to compete. He was there to win.

He was there to have his cake and, well, to eat it, too.

Mauna Kea and Mauna Loa, the ominous volcanoes responsible for this black rock in the South Pacific, could be seen clearly on the cloudless day on the North Kohala Coast. They are still active, smoldering deep below the surface. Nicklaus was smoldering, too.

It wasn't from turning 60. Nicklaus hadn't given his 60th birthday much consideration. "When I was a kid I used to say, 'good gracious, I wonder if I'll live long enough to see the twenty-first century?' I think I felt more about turning 40 than I did anything else. Turning 60 I don't think is that big of a deal."

He may have believed that from the standpoint of his golf career, but 60 was a significant milestone in the Nicklaus family. Neither his grandfather nor his father, Louis Charles and Louis Charles Jr., had lived as long. Jack became just the third male in the family to realize the age.

He accepted the celebration in good humor and bowed again when a traditional Hawaiian maile lei was placed around his neck. He was genuinely tickled when his playing partners, John Jacobs and Gary McCord, free-spirited Arizona neighbors, appeared tooting noisemakers and wearing brightly colored, pointed cardboard party hats, the kind held in place with a thin elastic band. Nicklaus removed his baseball cap with the Golden Bear logo and donned one of the hats. He readjusted it over his nose, drawing laughs. A chocolate-iced cake in the shape of the Big Island and adorned with candles awaited his attention.

"This will set your career back 60 years," Jacobs bellowed. "But that means you get to start over."

He *was* starting over.

He seldom had been more anxious about his golf game this early in the year, perhaps not since 1980, when he changed his golf swing after his first winless season. That campaign had turned out grandly, with two more major titles. Could he reprise those results? Certainly, he wanted it just as badly now as then—so badly that all the combustible desire churning inside had to find some kind of release valve. It finally did, the way it had for 40 years, manifesting itself into a fever blister that split the middle of his lower lip.

"When I'm keyed up and I start to put pressure on myself because I really want something in the worst way, bam! It just hits me," Nicklaus described with a wave of his hand over his mouth.

It didn't happen very often.

"I used to get them about four times a year," he confessed slyly, winking.

Four times. Rifle through the archives of the major championships over the last 40 years. Scrutinize the pictures of the omnipresent Nicklaus. Did you see it? It's there all right. Perhaps not every time, but it's there: the split lower lip. The man felt pressure after all. As his competitors usually discovered, however, the Nicklaus golf game rarely needed salve, especially down the stretch with a major title in the balance. When the heat was on, Nicklaus was reaching for Chapstick while everyone else was fumbling for a tourniquet.

Golf is a raw confession. The golfer's heart, soul, senses and his sins all are left vulnerable to barbaric assessment. That is the essence of the game's difficulty: attempting to control one's self while accepting the absolute and unavoidable betrayal of the self.

Nicklaus realized this long ago. You can talk about his powers of concentration, his ability to dissect a golf course, his excellence with the long irons and overwhelming advantage off the tee. They all were products of a central skill.

"I think my management of myself was probably stronger than the management of my golf game," Nicklaus said. "The golf courses were always there and I can manage those. Those are pretty static; they don't move around a lot. The human body and the human mind are much more complex. I think I managed myself pretty well and that was the important thing. It was focusing in on what I wanted to do and what I needed to do. Having the discipline to not try things I didn't think I could do. Make something happen when I needed to make something happen. All those things are what led to most of my success."

After essentially 18 months away from the game, Jack Nicklaus wasn't certain how much betrayal he was willing to endure, or would be forced to endure. The time to find out began when Hualalai's head professional, John Freitas, introduced him on the tee. (Typical of the modern era of sports, the tournament, broadcast by ESPN, began on the back nine to accommodate television.)

"Celebrating his 60th birthday, please welcome Jack Nicklaus," Freitas bellowed.

"I feel every bit of it, too," Nicklaus, wearing blue slacks, a light blue shirt and white and blue hat, deadpanned as he stepped behind the ball to unleash the first drive of a new century, the first drive in his drive to play again as he had in the previous century. He wasn't kidding, though, about feeling it. His back was acting up a bit, he was wearing heavy custom-made shoes with odd insoles designed to alleviate pain in his feet, and he was wearing magnets on his left hand, which was sore, he suspected, from his heavy practice routine.

He set up over the ball carefully, just as carefully and methodically as he ever had. He swung the club and watched the ball fly obediently down the middle of the fairway on the long par-5 hole, measuring 566 yards. It stopped 280 yards away. His second shot was equally good and his third, with a wedge, came to rest 20 feet from the hole. Two putts later he had a par, and he started a trend.

Five hours later, when the last of his two putts on the final hole dropped, Nicklaus had posted a two-bogey, one birdie 1-over-par 73. As he walked off the green his piercing steel blue eyes met those of his wife. "I pitched a perfect shutout today," he said, referring to the 36 passes he made with his putter. "It was a pretty boring round of golf," he later added stoically.

For the alacritous Jacobs, the defending champion, it was far from boring. "I only get fired up for two guys: Jack and Arnold," he said after muscling his way to a 64 and the first-round lead. His good friend and fun-loving accomplice McCord, meanwhile, tried to write himself further into dubious golfing lore.

The irreverent CBS golf broadcaster was two under par through 13 holes when he shanked a 2-iron into the black, crusty and jagged lava at the 205-yard downhill par-3 fifth. Jacobs volunteered to assess the playability of the shot and walked on ahead. McCord thought nothing of Nicklaus also leaving the tee until he watched with dread as Jack followed Jacobs onto the rocks.

"The situation reeked of infamy," said McCord with more seriousness than is his penchant. "I've got Nicklaus up in the lava looking for a ball I shanked in there and I'm thinking to myself, 'Oh, great. What if he falls and breaks his hip? I'm going to add to my legacy. Kicked out of the Masters. Ended the career of the greatest golfer who ever lived.'"

Legends do not celebrate birthdays. They merely mark the time. Reluctantly.

Cutting any cake would have to wait while Nicklaus sliced up the Hawaiian turf in search of a more reliable swing. He exhausted several hundred balls, mostly with his driver, and waited out all but one player on the practice range, Gary Player. But whereas the diminutive South African lingered equally long on the practice putting green, Nicklaus eschewed the flat stick in favor of long ball lessons. "Putting doesn't mean diddly if you can't drive the golf ball," he said, harkening back to a philosophy that originated in boyhood. "I'll spend three hours with the driver and two minutes putting if I have to. If you can drive the golf ball, you can play."

He would, literally, drive home the point with a second-round 80. The Bear was in his usual ornery mood—he is a hall of fame needler—when he met playing partner Bruce Summerhays on the first tee. After taking one look at his driver, a Ping ISI with a gargantuan clubhead, Nicklaus smirked, "How does it do in the wind? I mean, can you get it to the ball?"

As winds gusted up to 30 miles per hour, Nicklaus struggled to get it in the house. He hit just seven fairways, suffered two triple-bogeys and incurred a two-stroke penalty for hitting the wrong ball out of the lava on the par-5 fourth hole. Nicklaus plays a Maxfli Revolution with

"JACK" stamped on it, all in capital letters. The ball he hit was a Revolution, but his name wasn't on it. He hadn't committed such a transgression, he reckoned, in more than 30 years.

Despite that two-hour range session the previous evening, Nicklaus had made no discernible progress, at least nothing that stuck. Even watching his swing briefly on videotape hadn't helped; he struggled to assimilate the visual lesson. Experience suggested the necessary correction was infinitesimal. The week after Christmas Nicklaus had been striking the ball beautifully. Now, well-struck shots and the reassuring feeling that comes with them, had vanished.

Aside from his company, this is where Nicklaus most misses Jack Grout, his teacher from Scioto Country Club since boyhood. Grout, who died in 1989, wasn't overly technical with his instruction, and his solutions were consistent with that philosophy. "I'd have a problem and he wouldn't say a word," Nicklaus recalled. "He'd watch me hit a few balls, maybe move my left hand over a hair and say, 'Why don't you go play a few holes and see how that works?' And, boom, the problem would be solved."

⌒

Instant solutions evaded Nicklaus as he completed his first individual tournament since the Novell Utah Showdown the previous August. He closed with another 73 for a 10-over-par 226 total and tied for 34th place out of 37 players while another 60-year-old with a fake hip, George Archer, posted a 207 total and two-stroke victory. Nicklaus earned $8,625, enough to pay for maybe two-thirds of a tank of jet fuel for his Gulfstream III, which holds 4,200 gallons.

"I hadn't played my own ball in a long time. I'm rusty, obviously," Nicklaus reasoned. "I knew it was going to be hard, but I didn't think it was going to be near that hard."

A few days later Nicklaus encountered the embodiment of how hard, uncompromising and downright cruel golf can be when he set out for a practice round at Mauna Lani Resort, just north of Hualalai, in preparation for the made-for-TV Senior Skins Game, and happened by Ian Baker-Finch, one of the most "dogged victims of inexorable fate," as celebrated author Dan Jenkins might refer to him.

Winner of the 1991 British Open, Baker-Finch was a part of the ABC Sports broadcast team working the Senior Skins. Baker-Finch, a lanky, handsome Australian, had retired from competitive golf in 1997 following a string of 32 straight missed cuts on the PGA Tour dating back to 1994. A short, straight hitter with a deft putting touch, Baker-Finch suffered the most severe case of self-immolation in recent golf memory following his two-stroke triumph over Mike Harwood in the 120th Open Championship at Royal Birkdale. In an attempt to increase his driving distance, Baker-Finch changed his swing and irreparably damaged his game.

Nicklaus already had a foursome, but invited Baker-Finch, riding alone in a cart, to join them on the South Course. Scott Lubin, Nicklaus' caddie and an assistant pro at The Bear's Club in Jupiter, Florida, and Jim Lipe, senior design associate for Nicklaus Design, teamed with Baker-Finch in a $5 Nassau against Nicklaus and Dave King, a friend and business associate of Gary Player.

The golf was loose and mostly forgettable the first few holes, except for the comedy of errors on the fourth hole. Within seconds, Nicklaus shanked a chip and Baker-Finch incurred a penalty for hitting Lipe's hand with a pitch from off the green while Lipe was marking his ball.

Lubin, 29, a former junior hockey standout from Boston who has retained an imposing build and often is mistaken for one of Jack's sons, inadvertently altered the tenor of the outing when he snap-hooked his drive into the lava on the par-4 fifth hole. Baker-Finch shuddered just looking at the offending ball flight; that was the shot that ruined him.

"That's the scary shot when you're in a tournament," Baker-Finch said. He smiled awkwardly. "I used to stand up on the tee sometimes and then back off and start waving people back," he revealed, waving his arm to mimic a clearing out motion. "I'd say, 'A little more on the left, please. Thank you. No, a little more. Don't lean in. Thank you.'"

The group laughed nervously and Lipe quickly changed the subject to golf clubs. Golfers don't dare allow snap hooks to seep into their consciousness. But an unmistakable air of concentration now permeated the outing.

On the seventh, a downhill par-3 of 201 yards, Nicklaus laced a 5-iron to within eight feet of the flagstick. Baker-Finch, with a 6-iron, topped him, knocking it to within three feet. As he walked off the tee, Baker-Finch confessed that while his iron game was solid, there was no carryover in confidence to his driver.

"Ian, your swing is too good," Nicklaus said before sharing with him a swing thought that he himself was working on.

Nicklaus had been attempting to get more of his right hand into the golf swing. "I've always said golf is a right-handed game."

Baker-Finch listened intently. He had heard just about every idea and swing tip imaginable during a five-year descent into golfing purgatory. A nugget of wisdom from the Golden Bear, the longest straight driver in the annals of golf, might signal salvation.

Sure enough, the first tee ball Baker-Finch struck was pure and straight. The second one he even faded slightly. "That's the way I used to hit it," Baker-Finch gushed excitedly.

Sensing the game was on, Nicklaus responded by slugging his tee shots with more authority. This continued through the remainder of the round, each man growing more confident by his respective progress. At the final hole Nicklaus and King, a 13-handicapper, stood poised to win the match despite being severely outmatched, but the Golden Bear, who owns the 18th hole of every golf course he has ever played, missed a three-foot birdie putt, allowing his three opponents to escape undamaged.

Baker-Finch, however, ponied up in another manner. Before leaving the green, he turned to Nicklaus, shook his hand warmly and paid him a touching compliment, saying, "Apart from coming back as myself in my next life, I'd want to come back as you." The remark elicited a slight smile and an almost imperceptible nod from the Bear. The tip from Nicklaus caused Baker-Finch to pause and reflect.

Baker-Finch remained greenside for several minutes, sitting in his golf cart and writing notes on his scorecard. "I have to write it all down to get it through my thick skull," Baker-Finch said, laughing slightly at himself. He admitted that he had given mild consideration to a comeback in the near future. Now that proposition, though frightening, seemed more realistic. Much like Jack Grout had done for him, Nicklaus provided Baker-Finch a small tip that produced big improvement and a ray of hope.

"That was a great day," Baker-Finch gleefully said with a wide grin creasing his tan face as he drove off.

In his championship years, essentially the period from 1962 to 1980 (he won 67 times on the PGA Tour in that span and placed among the top 10 in 236 of 358 events), Nicklaus seldom permitted his business ventures to encroach on tournament time. That changed with his evolution from golfer to golf course designer. In recent years, if geography worked in his favor, and sometimes when it didn't, he wouldn't hesitate to make a site visit immediately before or after a tournament. In 2000 it was standard procedure.

After the MasterCard Championship, Nicklaus devoted a day on the Big Island to one of his more than 70 ongoing design projects, Old Hawaii Golf Club of Hokulia. The Nicklaus Signature Golf Course is the cornerstone of a 1,000-acre residential and private club development masterminded by ubiquitous golf and real estate magnate Lyle Anderson, who owns Desert Mountain and Loch Lomond Golf Club, among other resorts.

More than 10 years ago Anderson paid $6 million for 2,000 oceanfront acres, the last available for development. He sold half of it to a Japanese consortium for $60 million. On the remaining tract Anderson planned to collect $5 million for each of the 40 one-acre lots set on bluffs overlooking the Pacific Ocean and sprinkled along the golf course.

"I'm in the wrong end of this business," Nicklaus observed with a laugh. "But Lyle has a knack for buying and selling property."

The two men, Nicklaus and Anderson, have a knack for collaboration. They have worked together on 11 golf courses. Anderson knows what he's going to get.

"People know it's Jack and it's going to be terrific," Anderson said. "You don't get surprises with Jack. You get great golf courses with a lot of value."

The Hokulia site is spectacular; perhaps one of the best Nicklaus has ever worked on, which is no small claim given that Nicklaus is particular about the sites on which he designs. There are numerous elevation changes and the coastal vistas are stunning.

But the parcel presented diverse architectural problems. Because Hokulia, which means "Star of Desire," sits between Mauna Loa and Mauna Kea, the prevailing trade winds bypass the property. Such unusual calm, though ideal for golfers, makes Nicklaus' task more challenging. "We'll have to work hard to keep the course from getting boring," he said.

However, the "makani," or lack of it, was a mere irritation compared to other considerations. The Ala Loa Trail, or Old Government Trail, a dirt path lined by lava rocks or in some places elevated with round stones carted hundreds of yards uphill from the beach by the Hawaiian natives more than two centuries ago, meanders throughout the property. State regulations forbade its removal or disturbance. The sacred Kuakini Wall, a three-foot high wall of stone running some 18 miles to Kailua-Kona, was a further obstacle. It was built in the 1840s to control the expanding cattle population. It is four feet wide, but in some areas it expands to seven feet and contains the remains of children who died during a mysterious flu epidemic. Ground above lava tubes, some serving as tombs for the ancient Hawaiians, also were designated untouchable by the state.

If that wasn't enough, the property also featured the remains of a mysterious so-called "Ghost Trail," an earthen track barely visible. It was protected by an edict of the local town council until Anderson lobbied strenuously for relief from the restriction, arguing logically "ghosts can go wherever they want." Unable to conjure up a suitable rebuttal, the town council, after considerable stalling, relented.

The regulations protecting these landmarks and edifices stifled creativity. The result: a site visit scheduled to last a few hours became an all-day quest for solutions. Nicklaus and his team altered entire holes—the third, fourth, 17th and 18th—and tweaked several others. A metamorphosis of architectural philosophy ensued. With Anderson's urging, Nicklaus eliminated 70 of the nearly 100 bunkers in the original plans and replaced them judiciously with monkey pod trees. The most nettlesome problem was the routing of 17 and 18. The Kuakini Wall and several lava tubes made completion as originally intended impossible. The group was stumped for more than an hour on how to proceed.

"This is where Jack is at his best: problem solving," Dick Frye, Anderson's vice president, whispered to an observer.

Eventually, Nicklaus sketched out entirely new holes, changing the 3-5 finish to a couple of stiff par-4 holes. "Let's build a golf course that fits the land," he reasoned. Anderson, who was preparing to meet with deep-pocketed prospective members immediately after the marathon session, nodded his approval. He looked pleased.

Nicklaus pumped a fist, then backhanded himself a compliment. "I didn't know I was that smart."

The Skins Game was introduced to television viewers during Thanksgiving weekend in 1983 and became an instant, unparalleled success for several reasons, including a format mysterious to most of the sporting public and four participants who were the mainstays of golf: Palmer, Nicklaus, Player, and Watson.

Cable television and ESPN were in their infancy. Pro football was about the only TV fare available for millions of housebound fathers. Skins Game creators Don Ohlmeyer and Barry Frank theorized that golf, useless post-Labor Day programming in the eyes of the broadcast networks, might possess a certain attraction, especially to folks in northern climates, if the game's regal giants convened in an idyllic location and competed for sizable coin in an intriguing format.

Good theory.

The inaugural Skins Game was held November 26-27 in Scottsdale, Arizona, at Desert Highlands, a golf course designed by Nicklaus. Skins offered a then-obscene purse of $360,000. Palmer, not surprisingly, was the crowd favorite, and electrified his Army by grabbing a $100,000 skin and earning $140,000. Player, however, topped the foursome with $170,000, even though his seven skins were one less than Arnie's total. Nicklaus had two skins worth $40,000 and Watson took one skin and $10,000. The difference was Player sank a birdie putt worth $150,000 on the 17th hole, a huge payoff in an era when first-place in a PGA Tour event paid, on average, $70,000 and a Senior Tour triumph was worth about $25,000.

The high stakes made for powerful drama. Skins received an unexpected boost of validation when Watson vociferously accused Player of cheating. The program picked up a respectable 5.0 Nielsen rating, meaning it reached 4.1 million households. The following year, Nicklaus, less than two weeks after arthroscopic knee surgery, won $240,000 with a birdie on the final hole, the biggest check of his career to that point. Skins scored big, too, with a 6.3 rating, second only to the Masters among all golf broadcasts.

The upshot of the success of the Skins Game was the onset of what is now known as the "Silly Season." Predictably, as the game's legends aged and as the Senior PGA Tour established a foothold in the sports marketplace, there had to be a Senior Skins Game. It debuted in 1988. Two years later, when Nicklaus turned 50 and entered, the Senior Skins Game rated higher than its predecessor. In fact, from 1990-95, Senior Skins attracted more viewers four of the six years.

A reunion in 2000 of the four original Skins Game competitors seemed like a bright idea. Player, 64, remarkably fit and equally loquacious, predicted great things from the gray foursome. "Mark my words there are going to be some fireworks," he said. He did not mean the kind that percolated out of Watson 17 years before.

Nicklaus wasn't thinking of reunions, fireworks or his fellow legends when he stole away to the back end of the driving range at Mauna Lani on the eve of Senior Skins. Protected from strong winds by mounds on either side, Nicklaus hit balls in solitude, a luxury he seldom enjoys, and fixated on fundamentals.

"I have a lot of work to do before I feel comfortable," he said. "Right now I'm not comfortable with much in my game, but I'll get there."

There wasn't just hope in his voice. There was confidence, intent, and even contentment. He was enjoying himself. It had been so long since he could stand on a range and beat balls without discomfort. In fact, one year ago plus a day, on January 27, 1999, Nicklaus had his hip replaced. Less than 24 hours after the operation he forced himself to take a few tentative steps in a walker.

You bet he was enjoying himself, now that he no longer had to compromise his swing for a Pavlovian jolt from an aching joint.

"The last year being away from the game Jack found out how much he loves it," Ken Bowden, his friend and biographer, said. "I think in that regard he's more like Arnold than he thinks he is."

Still, the fabric of golf is an ill fit for Nicklaus unless he can tailor it to his ambition, which has never wavered from winning. "It's fun when you hit golf shots the way you want to hit them," he pointed out. "Arnold likes to be a part of what goes on and we all enjoy that to some extent. But I more enjoy playing good golf."

Just what good golf was supposed to look like in the whistling trade winds was hard to figure out. But like Ben Hogan, Nicklaus could find answers in the dirt. He checked and rechecked his balance. He worked on his rhythm and mechanics. The direction of the ball flight wasn't as important as its height. The path of his divots told him everything he wanted to know about the quality of his aim. He went through his bag methodically, starting with a 9-iron, then working to the 7-iron and 5-iron. After 20 minutes he switched to his 3-iron. The first swing induced a shout of glee from a giddy Golden Bear as it soared high in the air.

"Look at that 3-iron," he exclaimed with unabashed boyish exuberance. "I haven't been able to do that in a long time. That's what a 3-iron is supposed to look like in the air."

He struck a few more, then, emboldened, pulled out the 1-iron. "All right," he said, "time to put it to the test."

The 1-iron, with approximately 15 degrees of loft, is the most difficult club to hit consistently well. One of Lee Trevino's favorite lines is that when lightning is in the vicinity he likes to hold up a 1-iron, "because only God can hit a 1-iron." With the development of fairway metal woods and utility clubs, few of today's PGA Tour players put a 1-iron in their bags.

Nicklaus, however, at the height of his powers, wielded the 1-iron with alarming proficiency. It is still a club he relies on a great deal, though occasionally, depending on course conditions, he will trade it out for a 4-wood.

Three of the most memorable and magnificent shots of Nicklaus' career came while his hands interlocked on the grip of a 1-iron. In chronological order (and inverted order according to their significance): the 238-yard approach to the final green at Baltusrol in the 1967 U.S. Open; the near ace at the par-3 17th hole at Pebble Beach, the 71st hole of the 1972 U.S. Open; and the 242-yard second shot to the par-5 15th in the final round of the 1975 Masters.

Nicklaus often has called the last of these the best full shot under pressure he ever struck.

Considering this, you begin to understand the daunting task facing Nicklaus when he spoke of competing against himself. And you can understand when he says, "I look at my game differently than a lot of other guys. I'm so hard on myself."

He always has had to be. Look at the model he was attempting to emulate.

So now came a test, a pop quiz of self-examination. He swung the 1-iron smoothly. Contact was decent. He shrugged and nodded his head. Not bad. The second one was better. On the third…fireworks. The ball exploded off the clubface and climbed higher than his 3-iron.

With that, Nicklaus started singing. Yes, singing.

"Ooh-ee-ooh-ah-ah-ting-tang-walla-walla-bing-bang."

He reloaded. Another good one. A few more were equally well

struck. "If I can hit my 1-iron like that I'll use it more often," he said, beaming. He worked for five more minutes, cooled down with a few flip sand wedges, and packed up. "Good work today," he said, nodding with approval.

As he made his way to the club parking lot, his ebullience filled the cart. A man with a video camera approached. It was already turned on. "I wonder if you could say hello to my brother?" the man asked.

Jack obliged. "Hello to my brother," he said with a wry smile.

The man laughed so hard he nearly dropped his camera.

⌐

Any doubts Nicklaus may have had about his golf swing seemed to be quelled on the first hole of the Senior Skins Game the following morning. A solid drive and a monster 3-iron to three feet on the 533-yard, dogleg right, par 5 set up an easy eagle chance, which he converted. The remaining trio couldn't get inside him after three shots.

After tapping in, Nicklaus, who collected a $20,000 skin, announced, "Those are the kind of putts I like."

"You've had enough of them in your career," Watson retorted.

He just didn't have enough of them this day. Nicklaus was encouraged by his ball-striking, but he was far from satisfied. He won just one more hole, the par-3 seventh that he had played so masterfully a few days earlier. This time he nearly aced it with a 5-iron, the ball stopping 18 inches short on the 214-yard hole. The payoff was three skins and $70,000. It would be the last of his plunder.

Nicklaus continued to keep the ball in play, which made him look good on television, but only he knew how it was coming off the clubface. He wasn't thrilled. He wasn't giving himself many good chances and he finally let off a bit of steam on the 17th tee after yet another drive that wasn't all that it seemed. "I'm pulling out of it," he growled to Lubin. "I don't trust what I've got."

Nicklaus elaborated later. "When I'm trusting it I'm just hitting the ball and playing golf," he said before letting himself off a little. "I'm pleased for the most part. I hit some iron shots like I know what I'm doing. Last week I didn't have any idea what I was doing."

～

Nicklaus and his peers competed for $600,000, which none of them needs, and their performance suggested that the cash was of little consequence. Bragging rights figured heavily, which could be the only explanation for what occurred on a cloudless Saturday. The largest gallery in Senior Skins history—more than 10,000 people—assembled to witness a foursome who had given them so much in the past. Who knew they had more to give? Watson, the youngest man by 10 years, was expected to dominate, but the others, energized by the competition, responded to the challenge.

Taking a page from their past, each man displayed flashes of brilliance.

Watson won seven skins and $210,000. He birdied the last three holes in regulation. But it wasn't enough to win the day. Shades of '83, Player matched him down the stretch for halves, and dropped a fourth straight birdie on the group, from 18 feet, on the first playoff hole, the 196-yard par-3 15th to win four skins worth $220,000 and the title.

"We saw some great golf today," Nicklaus observed. "It was a pretty good TV show."

On the demanding 7,004-yard Mauna Lani layout, the foursome produced an impressive best-ball score of 60. They made eagle or birdie on 12 of the 19 holes. Not once did par win a hole.

"We've all competed against each other for so long and I think every one of us feels something special when we play together," said Palmer, who took three skins and $80,000. "We want to play as well as we possibly can when we're together and that's kind of what happened today."

～

As well as the four men performed on the golf course, it paled in comparison to their post-round press conference. The assemblage of four great golfers and, more significantly, four great sportsmen and speakers, was a poignant reminder that a quaint period in the game—in sport—had passed.

Each exudes a particular brand of eloquence in an individual setting. Seated together four abreast in the cart barn beneath the Mauna Lani clubhouse, which had been converted into a cramped, makeshift media center, they exhibited a comfortable familiarity with one another that bred contempt for standard question-and-answer protocol.

Senior PGA Tour official Phil Stambaugh mediated the press conference and attempted to initiate a review of the day's events. Stambaugh asked Nicklaus about his club selection on the par-3 seventh and henceforth lost all control.

"It was a 5-iron, but it wasn't quite enough club. It was six inches short," Nicklaus, seated on the far right, smirked.

"Aw, come on, it was longer than that," Watson corrected. "It was two feet."

"Was it?" Nicklaus said. "Well, about a foot and a half, then."

"Let's not argue gentlemen," Palmer, on the far left, intoned, half-serious. "Let's get on with it."

(Laughter.)

Stambaugh tried to gain control. Forget about it.

"Arnold, then you won two skins at No. 9. With a sand wedge? Is that what you hit there?" Stambaugh asked.

"I did. (Pause.) And um…you know when you get old your memory goes."

"You made a 20-foot putt," Watson said, assisting.

"I remember," Palmer said, feigning annoyance.

(More laughter.)

"It was left to right in the hole. Perfect. Dead center," Watson said.

"Did you all get that?" Palmer said, looking to the 20 or so media members.

"Maybe it was 30 feet," Watson corrected.

"His memory is worse than yours, Arnold," Player shouted.

(Laughter.)

"I thought it was more like 10 feet," Palmer said.

"Whatever," Nicklaus interjected with a dismissive wave.

(Bigger laughter.)

An elderly woman, a volunteer who snuck into the press conference, felt like getting into the conversation. She asked Player about his last trip to Mauna Lani. Was it in '87 or '88?

Uh oh.

"I honestly don't remember what year it was," he admitted.

Palmer couldn't resist. "Gary, that's the first thing you've ever forgotten."

(Uproarious laughter.)

"That's from following you," Player retorted.

"That had to have been in the '90s," Nicklaus said. "I think I won on a playoff hole."

"That's right," Player said, nodding and trying to redeem himself. "You made one from clear across the green. I got a birdie on the 10th hole, which is a par-5 and he knocks in about an 80-footer for eagle."

"That was about 25 feet," Nicklaus said, fibbing.

(Uproarious laughter.)

"Let's not argue, gentlemen. Get on with it," Palmer said.

(More uproarious laughter.)

"Please," he added, "don't ask us anymore memory questions."

(Loud guffaws.)

"I love you fellas, but it's time to go."

And with that Palmer arose from his chair, shook hands respectfully with his trio of foes, and walked out. There was no lingering sentimentality as the other players also stepped down from the stage, exchanged goodbyes, and dispersed, having enjoyed the orchestrated journey down Memory Lane, but obviously casting a ready eye to the off ramp.

Just as well for Jack Nicklaus, who was looking ahead to his first PGA Tour start in nearly seven months. "Going into next week I feel like I'm gaining on things," he said.

◡

Historically, the Monterey Peninsula in late January and early

February is hardly the optimum locale to build a golf game or sustain any momentum that might have been acquired prior to arriving in Northern California. The beauty of Pebble Beach Golf Links and the surrounding Del Monte Forest can be inspirational no matter how many times one visits, which is why the AT&T Pebble Beach National Pro-Am continues to be one of the most popular stops on the PGA Tour. Too bad they have to try and play golf.

Cool temperatures, chilling winds and rain are the elements that make up what is famously known as "Crosby weather." The phrase, born during the time when Bing Crosby hosted his "Clambake," has charm, but its properties chafe.

Jack Nicklaus, who fell in love with Pebble Beach on his initial visit in 1961 during which he shellacked all contenders on the way to his second U.S. Amateur title, knows how wicked the weather can be on the Monterey Peninsula and how swiftly clouds and fog can scurry in from off the Pacific Ocean. He first played in the Crosby in 1962, won it three times (in 1967, '72 and '73) and his visit in 2000 would represent his 37th in one of his favorite events.

Recently, however, the Monterey Peninsula had been particularly dank and dreary, not to mention detrimental to conducting a golf tournament. Rain shortened the event to 54 holes the prior two years (the '98 event, in fact, was suspended after 36 holes and wasn't completed until August), and in 1996 it forced the first cancellation of a PGA Tour event in 47 years. Few were surprised when an afternoon deluge forced a suspension of the first round on February 3.

Rain and the accompanying chilly air presented two problems for Nicklaus, by far the oldest player in the AT&T field. First, though rain can make a course easier by softening greens and making them receptive to aggressive approach shots, it also makes it play longer. Pebble Beach, at 6,815 yards and relatively flat, isn't long enough to hassle the Golden Bear, but the other two courses in the rotation, Poppy Hills and Spyglass Hill, lined by sloppy, gnarly rough and much more hilly, are inhospitable layouts to play and to walk.

"Length is not a factor for these kids out here, but it's become a factor for me," he pointed out.

Second, a sore foot and an aching back, soothed by the warm Hawaiian climate, conspired to stage an uprising in the California cold, prompting Nicklaus to become a frequent visitor to the Tour-provided fitness trailer. In the house behind the Pebble Beach driving range he has rented for years, Nicklaus showed off the inserts he had put in his specially designed golf shoes. They were designed to alleviate the very pains he was suffering.

"I think they're fixing some things and creating new dysfunctions," he said. "I just hope these are short-term dysfunctions; I'm a little tired of the ones that hang on."

On the driving range prior to the tournament, Nicklaus found a spot next to Vijay Singh and began to stretch. "Argh," he growled as he held an iron over his head and leaned to the left. "That one hurt. I can't wait to do the other side."

"What's the matter?" Singh, who seldom pauses from his incessant practice, turned around and asked.

"I'm 60, that's what's the matter."

⌐

To understand the impact Jack Nicklaus has had on generations of sports fans, it is helpful to observe the effect he has on those who have the opportunity to get close to him. John Elway won two Super Bowls as quarterback of the Denver Broncos after a number of disappointing performances in pro football's biggest game. Carrying a one handicap, Elway can handle the nerves that come with playing golf in front of a large audience.

But playing in the same group with Nicklaus is nerve-wracking. Elway, partnered with Gary Nicklaus in the two-man Pro-Am, barely got the ball airborne off the first tee, clubbing a low scooter that traveled 180 yards. Cincinnati Reds all-star outfielder Ken Griffey Jr. encountered the same level of discomfort playing with the Golden Bear a few days later.

"It is difficult not to be in awe, and it's even more intimidating in his element," Elway explained. "What he's done in his career, it's just incredible. I found myself watching him a lot because he's an icon in the game. I'm like everybody else. I was just in awe."

"I was shaking out there," admitted Griffey, who should have been better forged by the fires of regular games with his Orlando neighbor Tiger Woods. "I couldn't get settled."

Griffey, paired with five-time Pro-Am champion Mark O'Meara, another neighbor from the exclusive Isleworth community, bombed the ball but sprayed it to all corners, good for the batting average, but bad for golf scoring. "The problem with this game," Nicklaus informed him, "is that we have to play all our foul balls."

Nicklaus didn't enjoy playing his foul balls, which were too many, followed by too many rolling balls. He completed a 2-over-par 74 at Spyglass on Friday with 31 putts and was the only player in the foursome who didn't have a birdie. At one juncture his son and partner, Steve, a 10-handicap capable of inspired stretches of golf, asked for assistance reading a putt.

"I haven't had a one-putt green yet and you're asking me?" Jack said with mock astonishment.

The second round at Poppy Hills began with a light moment but ended in equally frustrating fashion. After hitting the opening green in regulation, Nicklaus trotted over to his wife and dug a paw into her purse. He had forgotten to take the three pennies he uses for ball markers off the dresser drawers. "First time in my life I ever walked on a golf course without any ball markers," he said sheepishly.

Silly things like that happen to golfers all the time—even to Nicklaus. Before the final round of the 1975 Masters, arguably one of the most exciting major championships ever contested, Nicklaus absent-mindedly stepped onto the range in his street shoes.

The round at Poppy was certainly forgettable. Most are, especially to players who for years were spoiled by playing the Alister MacKenzie masterpiece, Cypress Point Club. Cypress ended its association with the event in 1991 and quirky Poppy Hills took its place. Jack carded a 4-over 76 that included just one birdie. That came at the par-3 15th hole, his 33rd of the tournament, when his 20-foot putt rerouted off a spike mark and in. Further darkening his day was Gary's 73. The younger Nicklaus had gone out in a brilliant 32 and was just five shots behind the leader, Singh. But he bogeyed the par-5 10th hole and made a five at the par-3 11th hole with four shots around the green. Jack winced and exchanged a sigh with Barbara as he left the troubling green, feeling the sting as both player and parent.

A 72 at Pebble Beach on Sunday, his best score of the year, left Nicklaus far shy of making the cut, though he and Steve, playing together for the 13th time, were one of the 24 teams to earn a berth in the final round. Nicklaus hit 14 of 18 greens in regulation but needed 32 putts. He couldn't even get the architect's roll. Nicklaus designed the new par-3 fifth hole, 188 yards, which opened in November 1998, putting yet another of his stamps on a golf course already so thoroughly marked by his presence. But after a 5-iron to seven feet, he lipped out the birdie.

"I'm a little disappointed in my play," Jack said. "My golf game is not very good. I know I have to be patient with myself, but I'm not very good at that. I don't know where I expected to be at this stage, but I should be further along than this."

Indeed, he thought he was building a golf swing in Hawaii. Instead he had constructed a sand castle that crumbled with the rising tide of golfing difficulty.

As the tournament concluded on Monday, the Nicklaus duo carded a 63—with Jack converting three birdies, as many as in his three previous rounds combined—and finished sixth. Steve wasted little time hinting that he would enjoy a return engagement, but he was resigned to the inevitable. "Never say never, but I think this is his last time here," he said.

Jack, who first played in the event with actor Bob Stirling and also teamed with former President Gerald Ford before Steve became his regular partner, declined to rationalize the future.

"If we played the whole tournament on this golf course I'd be back every year," he said. "The other courses are all right, they're just not Pebble Beach. There aren't many Pebbles. My nostalgia is for Pebble Beach and not the golf tournament. My time here is finished."

He wasn't quite finished. His spirit hung around.

Down seven shots with seven holes remaining, Tiger Woods rallied past rookie Matt Gogel with an 8-under 64 and captured his sixth consecutive victory, matching Ben Hogan for the second-longest streak in PGA Tour history. The phenomenal Woods holed a 97-yard wedge for eagle at the par-4 15th hole and covered the final four holes in four under par. Down the stretch Tiger adopted a philosophy that was simple, familiar, effective.

"When everything is on the line, you forget about how bad you played or how good you played. All that really matters is the moment," Woods said, recalling the words of another great player. "What really counts is right now."

Jack Nicklaus couldn't have said it any better. In fact, Jack Nicklaus had said something to the same effect several years before. It was after winning the 1986 Masters.

3

SPRING

RISING TO THE OCCASION

"The thing that sets golf apart from other sports is that it takes self-confidence, an ability to rely totally on yourself. When I'm through, I'll really miss kicking myself to get it done. I can live without the Masters. But the really satisfying time is the three weeks leading up to the Masters."

—Jack Nicklaus

In 1953, at his first U.S. Junior Amateur Championship at Southern Hills Country Club in Tulsa, Oklahoma, Jack Nicklaus received his first and only lesson in tournament punctuality when he languidly arrived 30 seconds prior to the start of his opening match. This near-tardy nonchalance prompted a scolding from the starter, Lee S. Reed, who harrumphed, "Mr. Nicklaus, another half minute more getting here and you would be on the second tee one down."

So Nicklaus learned to arrive early for his tee times, though he is notoriously late for practically everything else, circumstances he won't deny.

In stroke play, the penalty for tardiness is two strokes. Two strokes. They might just as well have been two daggers to Charlie Nicklaus' precocious boy. Two strokes? Such a thought was absolutely abhorrent.

But sons become fathers and viewpoints change. In the midst of the first senior major of the year, The Tradition, at Desert Mountain Resort in Scottsdale, Arizona, Nicklaus, now a father thinking of his own son, half-seriously contemplated such a penalty rather than miss watching his boy make a bid for his first PGA Tour victory. Two strokes. It was conceivable, except that Nicklaus would never allow himself to commit such an impropriety. There was a round of golf to complete, a tournament to finish, a quest to fulfill. So rather than watch Gary close out his third round at the BellSouth Classic in Atlanta on April 1, Nicklaus dragged himself from the lunchroom television and back out onto the chilly Cochise Course, where the third round of the Tradition was about to restart after its third weather delay. Nicklaus was the last player to leave the clubhouse and he budgeted no time for a visit to the practice range, where all the other creaky over-50 golfers were limbering up yet again.

"It was so much fun to watch," Barbara said, beaming. She had stayed in the clubhouse while Jack departed. "Jack watched Gary hit his tee shot on 18, then he's looking at his watch and he says, 'You know what? If I don't go now I'm going to be late. Should I watch the second shot? No, I better go.'"

Nicklaus and his caddie, Scott Lubin, sped in their cart to the 13th tee, one of the farthest points from the clubhouse. Gary, meanwhile, was leaving a birdie putt on the lip of the par-5 18th hole at the TPC at Sugarloaf. His 67 and 11-under-par 205 tied Phil Mickelson for the lead.

But Jack actually had seen enough—for inspiration. He birdied the 13th hole, a downhill par 3 of 146 yards, with a 9-iron and a snaking 25-foot putt. He pulled his tee shot at the par-4 14th and a tree inhibited his backswing, but Nicklaus managed to bump his ball short of the green, about 35 feet from the flagstick. From there he chipped in.

He had just saved himself two strokes. Two strokes.

"I went out there and was so charged up. I figured if my kid could do it I could do it," Nicklaus said afterward. He shrugged and grinned, but the unassuming gestures couldn't hide his pride.

He capped the day with birdie at the par-5 18th hole by blasting from a waste area behind the shallow green. The eagle attempt trickled to within inches of the cup. He played six holes in three under par and scratched out a round of even-par 72 after converting just three birdies in his first 44 holes on a course with five par 5s and on which he'd won four times in nine starts.

In the blink of an eye, three months of moribund play had all but vanished. A burden had been lifted; it was a stunning turnaround. After signing his scorecard, Nicklaus met with ABC on-course reporter Judy Rankin before happily facing an onslaught of television and newspaper reporters who were eager to talk about Gary.

"I'll talk to him in a little while and see how he's feeling. I'll say, 'Nice round Gary, do it again,'" Nicklaus said, effusing deep pride. "I'm always a nervous parent, so is Barbara, but we can't do anything more than be parents. Just as he's been on the sidelines rooting for me I'll be on the sidelines rooting for him tomorrow.

"It's his game, it's not my game."

The game Jack Nicklaus had taken with him six weeks earlier to the GTE Classic February 18 at the TPC at Tampa Bay in Lutz, Florida, was one he didn't recognize. He had played too long with that feeble hip to have any sensory recall of his foundation swing, the one that he had built and programmed with Jack Grout through three decades. Neither could he reproduce—nor did he want to reproduce—the manufactured pass he had concocted the last six to eight years to accommodate a left side that was incapable of supporting him or swiveling out of the way.

New hip. New man. New swing.

Since leaving Pebble Beach, Nicklaus had worked diligently but progress was lacking. "My golf game is not there yet," he explained on the eve of the GTE, which he won in 1996. "I haven't played golf for a couple of years, really, so it's going to take some time to get back to learning how to play golf."

One problem: he did not have the luxury of time. "I've always been very patient, but right now it's hard for me to be patient. Time runs against you."

Another problem: Not only was he toiling to find a swing, but also his knack for scoring. Bobby Jones referred to this as the battle with Old Man Par. For perhaps the first time since he was a teenager,

Nicklaus was losing the skirmishes. "I'll go out and play pretty well and shoot 70 or 71 and walk off the golf course thinking, 'How come I didn't shoot 65?' Or I'll shoot 75 and think, 'Seventy-five? I only missed a couple of shots. How did I shoot 75?'"

⤿

The TPC at Tampa Bay, designed by Bobby Weed, is one of the few courses on the Senior PGA Tour that Nicklaus enjoys and respects, "because you have to hit golf shots; it requires you to play very good golf." Though set up for the seniors at just 6,638 yards, the par-71 layout is fraught with peril: 81 bunkers and 19 water hazards.

Nicklaus walked off the sun-drenched course after the first round having allowed Old Man Par to slither away again. The Golden Bear was two under after a two-putt birdie at the par-5 12th hole. He was near the lead and poised to go deeper into red figures. Instead, he bogeyed three of the last five holes with an assortment of pulls and three-putts. It added up to 72, one over par, on a nearly perfect day for scoring. "I let it get away from me," he groused.

Barbara, adorned in a white sweater with a large playing card on the front—the Jack of Hearts, of course—worn to curry good luck, appeared more disappointed than her husband. She had been witness the past few months to the work Jack had applied to his comeback. He hadn't worked this hard in more than 10 years. "He's just getting nothing out of it," she sighed.

But the beauty of a score is in the eye of the scorer. A short time later another golfer came in with a 72. Arnold Palmer, 70, who at the beginning of the year received a lifetime exemption into senior events, was mighty pleased. "I had a good round," he said. "Maybe I found something."

If he had found something, he would have the chance the following day to show it off to someone who mattered to him. He and Nicklaus were paired together for Round 2.

⤿

Through the years Nicklaus and Palmer have shared hundreds of competitive rounds, with none more famous than their first showdown, in a playoff in the 1962 U.S. Open at Oakmont Country Club in Oakmont, Pennsylvania. Nicklaus, a chubby rookie from Ohio, was literally and figuratively cast as the heavy against the immensely popular Palmer, who enjoyed the seeming luxury of playing close to his home in Latrobe, Pennsylvania. With Nicklaus emerging victorious, 71-74, the usurpation of Palmer's reign began right then and there. However, it would take years for Nicklaus to be appreciated and respected. Palmer, who fit neatly in the cradle of TV, won the popularity contests even when Nicklaus won the tournaments. Throughout the years the pair engaged in the fiercest battles.

Nowadays the embers of their rivalry barely glow. The two men still want to beat each other, but they have been through too much together to stir much in the way of competitive emotion. Nevertheless, any occasion that pairs the giants still elicits wonder from those around them. For example, Roy Vucinich, the third member of the group, couldn't contain his enthusiasm. He phoned the tournament office three times Friday evening to confirm his playing partners were Palmer, his hero, and Nicklaus, his idol. "Wanted to make sure it wasn't a prank," he explained.

An estimated 50,000 people were in attendance on a brilliant and hot Saturday and most of them flocked to the King and the Golden Bear. The popularity of the Senior PGA Tour has been on the wane for a number of years, as Nicklaus and Palmer and Lee Trevino and Gary Player—the legends who justified the existence and spurred the success of the tour—have receded from the limelight. But the TPC at Tampa Bay was abuzz. Sure, the duo had just played together in the Senior Skins Game less than a month ago with Player and Tom Watson. No matter. Every round the two old foes share could be their last together, a last chance to relive some of golf's most heavenly days.

Nicklaus and Palmer began their round seven shots off the lead set by Jim Dent and Simon Hobday. By the end of the day they had lost ground to Bruce Fleisher, a second-year tour player who had won seven times in his rookie season. Fleisher, a cheerful and respectful sort who won the 1968 U.S. Amateur, posted just one victory in 408 starts during his PGA Tour days. In fairness, Fleisher's career might have been more sparkling if not for personal setbacks related to complications his wife, Wendy, experienced during the birth of their only daughter, Jessica, in 1980. Wendy slipped into a coma and was on life support for four months. Fleisher gave up the tour for seven years in exchange for a club pro job in South Florida. He won his only title at the 1991 New England Classic, and then slipped back into a middling tour existence.

His golf, however, had been exceptional since he turned 50. Thus, Fleisher became the latest example of the odd evolution of the Senior PGA Tour into something far less meaningful than its intended purpose and far more of a bonanza for clusters of marginal PGA Tour players. An entire generation of golfers who lived in the shadows of Palmer or Nicklaus and lost to them often has realized an immense windfall from an enterprise established and perpetuated on the basis of the duo's status and reputation.

If you can't beat them, join them.

For his part, the unassuming Fleisher recognizes this and accepted his continuing anonymity in the wake of the Big Two pairing. "If I were a spectator, I'd want to be there, too," he said.

The golf Nicklaus and Palmer offered was marginal, though no one but the players seemed to mind. Nicklaus perked up on the back nine for three birdies and handed in his first subpar round of 2000, a 1-under 70. Palmer, meanwhile, bogeyed the first two holes, never righted himself, and slipped to 77. Each man said it was enjoyable playing with the other—and meant it—while bemoaning his receding capabilities.

"It's always a pleasure to play with Jack," said Palmer, who has not won a tournament since the 1988 Senior Tour Crestar Classic. "My game showed itself today. I didn't play well."

"My golf wasn't very good," Nicklaus echoed. "Arnold and I had fun together. We're both out there trying to learn the silly game."

They persist despite the inevitable deterioration of physical skills. On the golf course their conversation seldom strayed from the subject.

"We always talk about our bodies. Neither one of us are happy with those," the Golden Bear admitted.

Afterward, on the driving range, they resumed their discussion. Nicklaus ventured to the end of the range farthest from the clubhouse, but after 30 minutes on the shadeless practice tee he took a break and joined Palmer. Soon they were dissecting Palmer's setup. The Bear thought he was bending too much from the waist, losing the relationship between his shoulders and knees, which should line up perpendicularly.

"As the round wears on you get like this," Nicklaus said. He held up his index finger and slowly crooked it.

"That happens to a lot of things on my body," Palmer replied with a mischievous grin.

Nicklaus winced. He paused to collect himself. "It (an improved stance) could get you back to the way you used to swing, around your body," he said finally. Palmer, however, struggled to straighten his back. Finally, he contorted his frame close enough and stung a 6-iron. Contact was clean, and the ball flew straight. Palmer glanced back at Nicklaus and grinned.

"I just don't know if I could do that all the time," Palmer said, pursing his lips.

Nicklaus returned a smile, nodded, then warmly put a hand on Palmer's shoulder. Though 10 years younger, he knows all about the ravages of time. Jack whispered something in his ear, patted Palmer's shoulder again, and then traipsed back to his own bag and his own golfing riddles. One could only wonder what two of the game's greatest players would share privately in that poignant interlude.

Nicklaus did not have his riddles solved sufficiently for the final round, in which he steered it around for a 71 with a "mechanical" swing. "It's simply a matter of going 1-2-3-4-5-6 and getting into all these positions in the phase of the swing, which I know I need to do for awhile. But pretty soon you have go play golf."

His 213 total placed him in a tie for 14th, but he was far adrift of Fleisher's 13-under winning effort. Nicklaus didn't care that he notched his first top 25 finish on the senior tour since a Herculean 18th place in his return to competitive golf the previous May at the Bell Atlantic Classic in Avondale, Pennsylvania. He wasn't altogether unhappy either.

"It's just mileage under my feet," the Bear assessed, accepting the reality that he had competed in just his ninth individual tournament in two years. "I need to build up the mileage and play more golf."

❧

The day after the tournament, on Monday, February 21, 30 years and two days after Charlie Nicklaus died of pancreatic cancer, his brother, Frank, succumbed to the same disease. The funeral was three days later in Naples. "It's almost eerie; two brothers, 30 years apart, being taken the same way," Barbara said.

"It's just something in the family," Jack said morosely. "It's something I'll have to look out for. Something for my kids…"

He didn't finish the thought. Didn't want to dare it. Mortal thoughts for one's own self are barely manageable, let alone considering the fate of your children—a parent's greatest fear.

Close on the heels of Frank's passing followed another jolt when John Montgomery Sr., the founder of Executive Sports and one of Nicklaus' closest friends, collapsed with an apparent stroke in the dining room at Doral Resort & Spa two days prior to the start of the Doral-Ryder Open. Jack and Barbara, seated at a table nearby, heard a sickening thud, saw Senior on the floor and rushed to his side. The Nicklauses accompanied him in the ambulance to the hospital.

Fortunately, it was a false stroke—syncope—and Montgomery was up and about within days. Asked about the experience, Nicklaus was philosophical and realistic. "You get to a point in your life where you expect more (bad) things to happen and I suppose I am now at that point," he said.

❧

The Doral-Ryder Open in Miami always has been a favorite Nicklaus haunt. Since it first appeared on the PGA Tour schedule as the oxymoronically named Doral Country Club Open Invitational in his rookie year of 1962, the Golden Bear had missed it just twice: in 1970, when he withdrew after his father died, and in 1999, though he made a cameo as a spectator to watch Gary. He has equal devotion among regular tour stops to just two events: the Pebble Beach National Pro-Am and his own Memorial Tournament.

Venue is the key. Doral, where he won in 1972 and '75, is among a handful of tournaments competed on the same course throughout its history. The Dick Wilson-designed Blue Course, more famously known as the Blue Monster, is a good one—one of those exacting challenges Nicklaus enjoys. You have to hit golf shots. Its convenient proximity to his North Palm Beach home, about 90 minutes, is a plus.

Nicklaus' appearance was his 37th at Doral and undoubtedly his least enjoyable in what would turn out to be the final edition sponsored by Ryder. Ryder pulled out after 14 years primarily because its once-glittering fields had been decimated by a beefed-up West Coast Swing, anchored by the $5 million World Golf Championship Match Play event at La Costa Resort and Spa in Carlsbad, California, the week prior. It didn't help that there was almost universal discordance over the redesign of the Blue Monster by Raymond Floyd in 1996. Only six of the top 20 players appeared at Doral. The tournament headliners were Nicklaus and three-time champion Greg Norman.

Battling back spasms and his circuits overloaded by advice from a host of well-meaning friends and tour players, Nicklaus shot a pair of 3-over-par 75s and missed the cut by nine strokes. In the first round, 75 players in the field of 144 broke par. In the second round, Stephen Ames from Trinidad and Tobago shot a course-record 61 and rookie Edward Fryatt, a Nike Tour graduate from Rochdale, England, tied a PGA Tour record with eight straight birdies in firing a 62. The Bear was one of just 23 players who didn't break par. Gary was another and was down the road with 75-74-149.

Jack hit just 15 of 28 fairways and 24 of 36 greens. He took 32 putts per round. He had nothing going as evidenced by three measly birdies over 36 holes. He was backsliding.

"I don't know why I've gotten as bad as I've gotten this year," Nicklaus said with befuddlement. In search of a bit of magic, he even experimented in Round 2 with a Kasco VS Force driver borrowed from playing partner Fulton Allem. "I just haven't played very well. I hit the ball a reasonable distance at both the Father-Son Challenge and the Diners Club Matches and (Tom) Watson said to me, 'I haven't seen you hit the ball this far in years.' I couldn't hit it past…my wife will get mad at me…but I don't think I could hit it past her right now."

In addition to the mounting frustration, Nicklaus seemed to be grappling with the onset of real doubt. He still had the magnets taped to his left hand. A writer asked if they helped. Nicklaus said no. Relief was required elsewhere. "I'm going to buy a thousand of them and put them on. Actually, I'm going to put one here and one here."

He pointed to either side of his head.

Still, ever the optimist—one of his most effective weapons, really —Nicklaus latched onto a glimmer of progress he had made over the final four holes, where he had outdriven Allem by 15-20 yards. "The last four holes I hit the best six full shots I've hit in a month," he said. "I think I'm going with that swing for awhile."

Whatever Nicklaus thought he had found had vanished by the time he returned to competition two weeks later at the 23rd Liberty Mutual Legends of Golf at the World Golf Village in St. Augustine, Florida.

Nicklaus had committed in October to appearing in only his second Legends of Golf after an invitation from Raymond Floyd, who also would be making just his second start in the two-man best-ball competition. Nicklaus also was fulfilling a promise to PGA Tour commissioner Tim Finchem, who had made a plea to Nicklaus to support the flagging tournament.

Floyd, over the years, had become one of Nicklaus' closest friends among players, perhaps because they share a mutual respect and similar beliefs on golf and life. Floyd and his wife, Maria, were among the 130 people who gathered for Jack's 60th birthday party in early

January at the simple but stately Nicklaus home in North Palm Beach, Florida. The Floyds earned the distinction of bringing the best gift, a book entitled, "Sex after 60."

Jack leafed through it once rapidly, and then shouted, "Barbara you have to read this."

"I don't have time," she said, smiling and laughing.

"Believe me, you'll have time," he assured her, giggling.

The pages were blank.

∽

The Legends of Golf, founded by Fred Raphael, the man who created the original golf travelogue series, *Shell's Wonderful World of Golf*, was first held in 1978 at Onion Creek Country Club in Austin, Texas. Televised by NBC, the Legends consisted of 12 two-man teams that included Gene Sarazen, Sam Snead, Jimmy Demaret, Jack Burke, Paul Runyan, Tommy Bolt, and Peter Thomson. Snead birdied the last three holes as he and Gardner Dickinson edged Thomson and Kel Nagle by one stroke. Two years later, with the Legends of Golf as the inspirational cornerstone and following on the heels of Arnold Palmer's 50th birthday, the Senior PGA Tour was formed.

The event enjoyed tremendous support and success in Austin, both at Onion Creek and, starting in 1990, at Barton Creek Country Club. But after moving to the PGA West Stadium Course in La Quinta, California, near Palm Springs, its popularity faded due to a lack of support from the snowbirds. A move to Florida's First Coast in 1998 wasn't the remedy either.

With Palmer landlocked in Orlando hosting his Bay Hill Invitational on the PGA Tour, only one man was capable of elevating the sagging fortunes of the Legends. And sure enough, after the Golden Bear announced his intentions to appear with Floyd, ticket sales doubled to nearly 50,000. Golden Bear, indeed.

Unfortunately, Nicklaus was far from in vintage form. His assessment of his golf game going in: "Horrible."

After the first round on The Slammer & The Squire Course,

Nicklaus' view darkened. Playing with Lanny Wadkins and Tom Watson, Nicklaus and Floyd shot a 68. Or rather, Floyd did. Nicklaus twice was in his pocket and did not contribute a birdie as the pair fell nine shots behind Andy North and Jim Colbert. "Lanny and Tom played very well. My partner played very well and I watched," Nicklaus said after a round of near total futility that he estimated added up to about 80. "I don't think I've ever played a worse round of competitive golf in my life."

Floyd wanted to help but didn't know how. "It's the chicken and the egg question," he said. "Do you get confidence from hitting good shots or do you hit good shots because of confidence?"

Nicklaus needed intense range work, but he didn't have the time. His lead design associate, Jim Lipe, had flown into St. Augustine so they could inspect The King & The Bear, the design collaboration with Palmer that would add a second course to the World Golf Village.

Forget the chicken. The word had been passed along to everyone on-site to walk on eggshells, so dour was the Bear's mood.

It didn't help that he and Lipe had to figure out a way to mesh the soft-flowing inclinations of their philosophy with that of the more dramatic movement preferred by the Palmer team. The course possessed two distinct personalities and Nicklaus wanted to soften some of the mounding and bunkers to preserve a semblance of a theme through 18 holes. The bunkers in particular were troubling. They were deep, steep-faced and jagged, with tortured fingering. They would be difficult to play out of and to maintain.

Developer Wayne Sloan preferred the understated style the Nicklaus team had created, but when one of the design associates mentioned that the Palmer Group had signed off on all the bunkers, Nicklaus, letting his sour mood get the best of him, replied, "Please respond that the Nicklaus Group thinks they look like shit."

That's when he spotted her. He had forgotten that an attractive, flaxen blonde, a girlfriend of the project manager, was sitting in the truck cab. She peeked out the back window, and as soon as he spied her, Nicklaus apologized for his use of vulgarity. The young lady laughed and assured him it was no big deal.

"But it is to me," Nicklaus said, continuing to apologize.

The incident served to illustrate the strict code of conduct to which Nicklaus adheres. A human being, Nicklaus is not above the occasional crimson expression, but he is well above loathsome behavior. Far from the public and with no more than a handful of people in his company, Nicklaus could do nothing but express immediate remorse for swearing in front of a lady, because that is his nature, his sense of decorum.

Nicklaus and Lipe reviewed nearly every hole and burned three hours before they felt comfortable with the layout. What made things go smoother than they otherwise might have was Palmer's input. He conducted a walk-through the week before and suggested about a dozen tweaks. Nicklaus approved of all of them and was delighted that his friend's ideas were more consistent with his own than he had surmised. He later called his collaboration with Palmer a pleasing success and one of immense enjoyment.

It was nearing sunset when Nicklaus, driving a white Lincoln, pulled out of the dirt-encrusted temporary parking lot onto a nondescript section of Highway 16A. He drove for a moment and then heaved a sigh. He confessed he was foundering in uncharted territory. He was lost at sea, helplessly adrift in that raft of uncertainty in which all golfers occasionally find themselves—even the great Golden Bear. But for the first time in his career, Nicklaus had misplaced the compass leading him back to the calming port of his abilities.

"I've gotten nothing out of my game, out of the work I've done and I don't understand it," Nicklaus said with bewilderment and dejection. "I have never gone through anything like this in my career."

It was a stunning admission from the player whose reputation was built on the confidence and solid management of his game. It also was a noteworthy testament to the game's unpredictability. Golf always is played alongside an invisible abyss. The most successful players avoid falling in or quickly extricate themselves if they do suffer a misstep. Nicklaus, like any other player, had had his travails, but never had his game fallen to such depths.

In the next breath, however, Nicklaus expressed optimism that he could at any moment regain his bearings. "I know I'm close, which just adds to the frustration," he said. "I will figure it out."

Throughout his career Nicklaus has benefited from top-notch instruction, starting with Jack Grout. Jim Flick, a business partner with Nicklaus in a series of golf schools, has done a reputable job as an erudite sounding board since Grout passed away.

The Bear also accepted tips from fellow pros through the years, though no one ever surpassed Deane Beman, the former PGA Tour commissioner, in dispensing bits of wisdom at the appropriate moment. On no less than four occasions—all at major championships—Beman, a one-time U.S. Amateur champion who won four pro tournaments in five years before taking the Tour reins in 1974, assumed the role of Nicklaus' pretournament savant, correcting a swing flaw here, giving a putting tip there. Beman possesses uncanny instincts and a considerable grasp of the game's fundamentals, which likely was the reason Nicklaus, no dummy, kept company with the diminutive but feisty player.

After contributing four birdies to a team 65 in the second round, Nicklaus, who lacked power in his shots, decided he couldn't tolerate another day of guessing. "What do you see out there?" he asked Floyd.

"I've hesitated to say anything," Floyd responded, "but you're coming in too vertical to the golf ball."

"Say no more," Nicklaus said, raising his gloved left hand. There was a slight gleam in his eyes as he headed for the driving range. Finally, a clue. A vertical swing plane he could get away with in his younger years, but it led to a loss of power as he aged. The result was an oblique strike on the ball, a glancing blow that lacked authority.

"I have to work on getting myself coming into the ball on a more shallow plane," Nicklaus explained. "If you read my book (*Golf My Way*)…I ought to be reading my own book…but that's what I say in my book."

Nicklaus hammered balls for more than an hour after the second round and the effort paid off Sunday when he shot a bogey-free 67 on his own. He and Floyd put together another 65 for a 198 total and tied J.C. Snead and Gibby Gilbert for ninth place. They earned $16,000 apiece. North, making his senior debut, and Colbert posted a wire-to-wire triumph with rounds of 59-66-66-191.

The only downside to Nicklaus' day was his continuing struggles with the putter. The mallet had become a sort of malediction. Better ball striking set up 12 birdie chances, but a seven-foot putt was the longest he converted. Nicklaus, no matter how disgusted he was with his short game, wasn't about to let that lingering problem overshadow the fact that he was on the verge of finding some kind of overall game.

"This gives me a little ray of hope with the direction I'm trying to go," he said.

When Nicklaus arrived at Desert Mountain for the Tradition, the subject of the Masters had not been broached often, and then only when others, mostly writers, queried him on the subject. He wouldn't deny it was in the back of his mind, but neither would he voluntarily talk about the tournament for the first three months of 2000.

That changed in the cool Arizona air.

The adjustments he made at the Legends were beginning to take hold through repetition, but they came at a price. His left knee began to ache the day after leaving St. Augustine and the pain had not abated in the days leading up to the Tradition. This prompted him to make a decision he absolutely detested. To ensure that he could cover the steep grades at Augusta National Golf Club, he opted to play out of a cart at Desert Mountain.

"For Jack Nicklaus to choose to ride in a golf cart is a significant thing," Flick noted.

Carts are permitted at all Senior PGA Tour events and co-sponsored events except the PGA Seniors' Championship and the U.S. Senior Open. Nicklaus and Palmer are among a handful of seniors who have abstained from riding, not only because walking is their preference, but also because they stubbornly hold firm in the belief that it is an integral part of the competition. It was a surprise to no one that the pair were summoned to testify on behalf of the PGA Tour in its legal scuffles with Casey Martin. A teammate of Tiger Woods at Stanford, Martin sued the Tour for the right to use a cart in PGA Tour tournaments under the Americans with Disabilities Act. Martin suffers from a rare circulatory illness in his right leg, which makes walking all but impossible for him. Unless a cure is found, loss of the limb is inevitable.

The Martin case was to be decided by the U.S. Supreme Court and initiated bitter debate in the golf world. Nicklaus and Palmer, defenders of tradition, unfairly took considerable public relations hits. Even as his hip degenerated Nicklaus continued to walk.

But now the Masters was a week away and it was too important to him to risk further injury. Tom Watson, 50, who had broken a bone in his foot jumping over a fence earlier in the year, opted to ride for the same reason. Augusta is a tough walk. And participants must walk.

〜

Nicklaus gave further evidence of his growing preoccupation with the Masters on the range after his opening round 1-over-par 73. The Bear produced two birdies to offset three bogeys, but he failed to birdie any of the five par-5 holes on the 6,959 yard Tradition course. "That's a sin," he said.

But his golf swing no longer was bedeviling him. "It looks smooth. It's no longer in three pieces," Scott Lubin gushed.

Better than the swing was the result. The trajectory of his shots was higher and curving predominantly from right to left instead of his preferred fade. After striking one high draw with his new Callaway Great Big Bertha Hawkeye driver, Nicklaus, smiling, turned to Flick and said, "That shot would work well at Augusta."

The trick was getting it to work in competition and he wasn't ready yet. His opening round on a warm, sunny and relatively calm day looked familiar and was discouraging. "I'm having trouble releasing the golf club. I'm afraid to release it."

And then there was his putting. Preparation for a major championship includes not only honing a swing and ball flight pattern, but also becoming completely comfortable with the equipment. After the Legends of Golf, Nicklaus exchanged his old N1 irons for an updated set also made by his Nicklaus Equipment Co. He also discarded the Kasco driver for the Callaway after testing nearly 20 Hawkeye Titanium drivers at home. But what to do about a putter? To win at Augusta, Nicklaus knew the putter would have to work, and work well.

In his struggles to rebuild his golf swing, Nicklaus had neglected his putting. Now it moved up the priority list. Augusta, with its lightning fast greens and pronounced curves and slopes, quickly would expose the weakness if he did not shore it up. He brought nearly a dozen putter models with him to Arizona and all would get a rigorous tryout. One putter absent was the oversized ZT Response, made by MacGregor, with which he won the 1986 Masters. In the days following Nicklaus' sixth green jacket, the odd-looking putter with the eight-inch face became all the rage. More than 6,000 orders poured in and MacGregor fell 10 weeks behind on production.

Before the Tradition, Barbara had asked Jack, "Why don't you go back to the ZT Response?"

"That's the one golf club I can't find," he said.

Turns out the putter disappeared a few years ago out of the club bin in their home. He sure could use it now.

"My putting is atrocious. I can't putt to save my life," he said. "That's kind of important next week."

Next week. Georgia most definitely was on his mind.

⌒

Inclement weather, a regular occurrence at Desert Mountain, interfered with Friday's second round. There was rain, lightning and chilling winds, which caused two suspensions in play lasting more than four hours. At least there was no snow, which hit in 1999 and forced organizers to reduce the event to 36 holes.

Nicklaus, playing with Dave Stockton and Dale Douglass, got in 14 holes Friday, then returned early Saturday to complete a second-round 75. Nothing much was happening, nor was he making anything happen on a course he had routinely plundered. In nine starts covering

35 rounds, Nicklaus had posted 25 rounds under par, including 18 scores in the 60s. In 1996, when he became the oldest Tradition champion at age 56, Nicklaus netted 20 birdies, one eagle, and a double-eagle at the par-5 12th hole on the way to a 16-under 272 total. His career stroke average on the Cochise Course was a miserly 69.77.

Saturday's third round was shaping up as equally uneventful. Lightning halted play yet again at 1 p.m. and it seemed like a merciful stoppage for the Golden Bear, who was 3 over par for 12 holes. The par-4 10th hole served as a microcosm of his round—of his year, in fact. At 424 yards, No. 10 is the fifth-longest par 4, yet Nicklaus reached it with a 9-iron. Then he three-putted from 20 feet for a bogey.

A black swirl of clouds that had hovered in the distance moved over the mountain as he completed the 12th hole. Soon sparks traced across the darkened sky, their might in contrast to the utter lack of electricity in Nicklaus' game. Until, that is, the jolt from Atlanta, from son to father.

The Nicklaus boys had always had this effect on the old man. They inspired him in ways that elicited the incomparable Nicklaus competitiveness. They'd be playing 18 holes and each knew where he stood in relation to his father. And, of course, Dad knew, too. He might be down a stroke or more heading to 18 but he would lay a Bear glare on them and let them, like so many opponents in so many tournaments, beat themselves. Or he'd need a 20-footer for birdie, line it up, and say something like, "Hate to do this to you." Then, like a smiling assassin, he'd gun them down, rolling in the putt.

"He was merciless," Barbara recalls. "They wanted to know how he could keep doing that to them. He even did it to me."

The only thing more brutal and savage was the games the boys played among themselves. They played against Dad for milkshakes or some such prize. The stakes were lower, uglier, and scarier in the sibling shootouts. Loser had to eat worms. Or worse.

Eventually each of the offspring, except for Nan, who didn't play golf, realized the ultimate conquest. Gary was the youngest to beat Jack, accomplishing the feat at 14. "I don't remember that," Jack said in mock seriousness when asked about the occasion. In 1986, it was Gary who assured his father prior to the Masters, "You're not that old." Gary also suggested his dad pluck the few rebel gray hairs that had invaded his blond sideburns that year.

Now Gary, with his fine play, was cajoling him again from long distance. And just like in all those private showdowns, Jack responded to the challenge. Building on the three-under effort over the last six holes Saturday, Nicklaus embarked on his best round of the year Sunday.

He went out in 34 by reaching both par-5 holes in two strokes. Meanwhile, Barbara was keeping abreast of the proceedings in Atlanta with the help of *Sports Illustrated* photographer Jim Gund, who was monitoring the NBC broadcast of the BellSouth Classic on a transistor radio.

As Nicklaus made his way to the 10th green, Barbara headed into the media center. The final round in Atlanta had been washed out and a one-hole playoff between Gary and Phil Mickelson was to begin in 15 minutes. She took a seat in the dining area and held her breath. Mickelson hit first and played a good shot about 15 feet left of the hole. The younger Nicklaus followed with an 8-iron that was right at the flag. But he had hit it a hair heavy and it splashed into the front bunker, perhaps no more than a foot from perfect. When he took two to get out, his fate was sealed.

His mom couldn't have been more proud. "My heart, my soul, my thoughts, my love, and my pride and everything are with him there," she said. "At least he was there. If you're not there you can't have a chance to win."

She was speaking from experience.

"Now it's back out to Dad," she proclaimed.

Dad was doing well. As Barbara left, Jack had felt his stomach tighten. It was in knots worrying over Gary. But he put the nervous energy to good use, birdieing 11 and 12. He was heading to the 13th tee when a man armed with his wife's pager informed him of the results. "I hope your wife's pager is wrong," he barked.

Barbara confirmed the outcome on the 14th fairway. "Well, he did great," he said to her and gave her a peck before going on to a solid and satisfying finish.

"Obviously, I'm very proud of Gary," Nicklaus said. "He may not have won the tournament, but he won a lot of things today."

Indeed, as a sign of the new era of largesse in golf, the younger Nicklaus collected $302,420, boosting his earnings to $348,420—more than his father pocketed in any one year. In 1972 Jack earned a career-high $316,911, but it required seven PGA Tour victories.

As omens go, the outcome was heartening for Gary. After all, Jack lost his first playoff to Bobby Nichols at the 1962 Houston Classic. A month later he beat Arnold Palmer in the U.S. Open.

⤸

When his last putt dropped, a four-footer for par at 18, Nicklaus had fashioned a 5-under 67, his first sub-70 score in nearly two years and the second-lowest round behind Howard Twitty's 66. By playing the last 24 holes in eight under par, Nicklaus climbed into a six-way tie for ninth place, his first top-10 finish in any event since July 12, 1998, when he placed sixth at the Ford Senior Players Championship. As Lubin extended his hand, Jack accepted it and took a step forward and said softly, "Hey, I finally got you a bonus check." Typically, players give their caddies a bonus, perhaps 5-7 percent, for a top-10 finish; a win might earn a caddie a 10 percent pop. Nicklaus awarded Lubin with a 10 percent pop from his $37,066.67 check.

"I thought, 'Oh, my gosh,' " Lubin, said. "With all he's got going through his head, that's the last thing he needs to be thinking about. But that's him."

Nicklaus did not stay for the completion of the tournament, which ended with a three-man playoff. In a battle of major championship winners, Tom Kite outlasted Tom Watson and Larry Nelson with a birdie on the sixth hole of sudden death.

An hour after he holed out, the Golden Bear was aboard Air Bear, bound for home. He was buoyant. He cranked up his favorite compact disc and Frank Sinatra bellowed loudly overhead. Nicklaus sang along with a mischievous grin as Barbara shrank from the decibel level.

Gary's performance, which all but locked up his PGA Tour card for 2001, had made him proud. His own efforts made him optimistic.

He had reason to be buoyant.

In almost mystical fashion, Nicklaus had conjured up a reasonably competent game. Augusta, one of his two favorite *places* in golf, was just over the horizon and the Golden Bear had been rousted from his slumber. It was almost as if there existed a synchronization of his flowering game and the blossoming of southeast Georgia azaleas, magnolias, and dogwoods—a cosmic cross-pollination.

"I'm not even sure how it happens," Nicklaus, slicing out a few divots from a carton of butter pecan ice cream, admitted, his mood nearly exceeding the altitude of his Gulfstream III with the code letters N1JN. His steel blue eyes were practically incandescent.

The mere thought of Augusta stirred Nicklaus. Once again he was becoming that man in spring. Autumn was withdrawing. Winter was held at bay.

"I still get excited driving down Magnolia Lane," he admitted. "The place excites me. I love the place."

And the place reciprocates. It wraps its leafy arms around him and fills him with confidence and the kind of hope that can only spring eternal in a blessed, select few.

"I feel like I can be decent, like I have a chance to do something now. I haven't felt that way very much this year. Well, not at all, actually."

He shrugged. "We'll see."

There are mysterious openings that develop in our lives. All we really know is that we should step through them and be ourselves.

Passing through the majestic gates of Augusta National Golf Club, who better to be than Jack William Nicklaus?

4
ECHOES
MAGIC MOMENTS AT THE MASTERS

"If I could just putt. I might just scare somebody... maybe me."

—Jack Nicklaus, 1986 Masters

He stood nearly motionless on the 11th tee and fixed his gaze down the fairway for an awkwardly long time. Where to hit it? Jack Nicklaus didn't know. Augusta National Golf Club is one of his two favorite places in golf. How many rounds had he played there? Officially, 152 prior to the 2000 tournament, but he had completed hundreds more in practice—and another several hundred in his macroattentive mind.

Until his 1999 absence, Nicklaus had competed in 40 consecutive Masters tournaments. In that span the course had undergone myriad transformations—new bunkers, new tees, different grass on the greens. (Nicklaus even had a hand in some renovations, which isn't saying much since nearly a dozen men have touched up the work of Alister MacKenzie and Bobby Jones.) But, strategically, it had changed hardly at all. No one knew the course better than the six-time champion. He seemed to be in tune with how every blade of grass stood, where the shade fell, where the air found the windows through the dogwoods and pines.

This was *his* place—*was* his place.

Now he stood on the 11th hole with not a clue where to aim his tee shot. It was late Tuesday afternoon, April 4, and Nicklaus was among the last players to embark on a practice round two days before the 64th Masters. The sun was out, but a constant breeze added extra nip to the cool air. Aaron Baddeley, the 18-year-old Australian phenom, edged closer when Nicklaus leaned in his direction. Baddeley held his driver out in front of him, pointing to a spot, a tree in the distance. *There* was the line. The other member of the group, Greg Norman, who had played in 20 Masters himself, listened intently and looked off in the distance to get his own bearings from Baddeley.

"You're sure?" Nicklaus, his face pallid, his voice filled with doubt, said haltingly.

"I'm positive," he replied. Baddeley, who had defeated Norman down the stretch at the 1999 Australian Open, had played a mere four rounds at Augusta National. Yet there he was, instructing two men who had competed in a combined 60 Masters tournaments.

"He's positive," Nicklaus echoed loudly to the gallery that stood three deep around the tee. They laughed a little. Then Nicklaus added, swiveling his head, "Sorry, I've never been here before."

So he hadn't. Think of how unsettling that must have been. Was he disgusted? Probably. Distraught? Almost certainly. Disappointed? You had better believe it. Hadn't the men in green jackets ever heard of New Coke? It is simply foolhardy to change the recipe of a classic.

The installation of rough, a "second cut," in Masters terms, was the source of Nicklaus' confusion and consternation. The growth was a mere 1⅜ inches, not high enough to prevent a player from reaching the green, but more than enough to prevent him from stopping the shot once it arrived. The longer grass impeded clean contact between the club head and the ball, which made it difficult to spin a shot, and, thus, hold the hard and slick greens.

"That was crazy, wasn't it?" Nicklaus said later, shaking his head when he recalled that awkward moment with the young Australian amateur. "That pretty much said it all."

It certainly did. After 41 years, Augusta National Golf Club finally had Jack Nicklaus stumped. He had applauded the addition of rough in 1999 when he took a tour of the grounds in a golf cart with new club chairman Hootie Johnson. But under the direction of architect Tom Fazio, Masters officials let the long stuff encroach further into the playing areas after '99 until all that remained of the fairways were narrow, arbitrary strips. The most severely narrowed holes were Nos. 1, 2, 3, 9, 10, 11, and 15.

Because the 11th fairway rises before trundling toward Rae's Creek, which runs behind the 11th green and in front of the 12th, the landing area is obscured. When all the grass was mowed to fairway length this was not an issue. It didn't mean accuracy wasn't important. Nicklaus shaded his tee shot to either side of the fairway depending on the location of the pin. That was how one played Augusta National Golf Club.

"You always played for the angles," Nicklaus noted.

It was a strategic charm MacKenzie and Jones had to have conceived from the beginning. But that charm had been eliminated. The only option at 11 was a laser down the middle of the landing strip fairway. That left the player a downhill approach Nicklaus classified as marginal as it relates to optimum angle into the narrow green. This was just one example of the course's character being grossly compromised. The most egregious example was at the par-5 15th, where trees on the left blocked half of the allowable driving area.

"They've taken the golf out of your hands now. It doesn't make any sense. No sense at all," he said. "Bobby Jones wanted a second-shot golf course. He loved St. Andrews and that style of golfing, but they've changed the nature of the golf course."

As late as two weeks before the tournament Nicklaus had continued to applaud Augusta for such alterations—until he got a closer inspection. He played a practice round March 22 with his son, Jack II, who would caddie for him, and club members Roy Simkins, a land developer, and Billy Morris, the publisher of the *Augusta Chronicle*. Nicklaus was disheartened to find the rough arbitrarily grown rather than trimmed along the tree lines to preserve the layout's natural routing. The course was lengthened, too, to 6,985 yards, the greens at 10 and 16 rebuilt, and there was new grass on 12 and 13. Trees were added at 14 and 17. To those changes Nicklaus had no objections, and he continued to praise Masters officials for the splendid condition of the course.

He got around in 78 strokes and joked to Barbara the next day, "I didn't realize they lengthened every hole by 20 yards."

But that one sticking point was critical in his mind.

"I don't like what they've done to the golf course at all," Nicklaus said shortly after that visit. "They've taken a golf course played for years a certain way and now they've eliminated that. I was in favor of them putting in the light rough, but I didn't realize they did what they did. I thought it was on the shape of the fairways and the shape of the holes that brought light rough into play on the errant tee shot to make it hard to pick the ball up and make it stop on the green.

"It looks like somebody who doesn't play golf or understand the game did it, and I've never said that about Augusta before." It was the first time Nicklaus had let such a personal thought become public.

Nicklaus' condemnations were far from cries in the wilderness.

Two-time winner Ben Crenshaw, himself a respected architect, was just one of the many veterans who joined the Bear in expressing bewilderment over what had been done. "The golf course was virtually a new golf course," he said after the tournament. "You understand why they did what they did, but it no longer was Alister MacKenzie's golf course and I have to believe that it played in no way that Bobby Jones intended."

Tiger Woods, who won by 12 strokes in 1997 and set the 72-hole scoring record of 18 under 270 (eclipsing by one shot the mark shared by Nicklaus and Floyd) didn't understand the club's logic. "It's such a great golf course," he said. "I don't see the need to change it every year. I guess it's something they like to do around this place. Maybe they're bored."

The growing of rough had been instituted ostensibly to put a greater premium on driving accuracy. That decision was based on the assumption such premium was absent before. On the contrary, Nicklaus understood that Augusta has always demanded precision golf to maximize birdie opportunities. And who had proved to be the best at that?

With the exception of the par-5 holes on the front nine, which he could no longer reach in two shots, Nicklaus had played Augusta National the same way for 40 years. He won the Masters six times, finished second four times, and posted 22 top-10s playing it his way. Now he had to play it someone else's way.

On the previous morning, Monday of Masters week, Jack had slept in, no doubt dreaming of another glorious week in Georgia. Clad in a gray T-shirt and shorts, he didn't reach the breakfast table in his Florida home until 9:30 and by then Barbara had been up for 2½ hours. She already had worked out and caught up on the mail. A number of newspapers were laid out and Jack dug in while eating half a cantaloupe. First he read the accounts of the BellSouth Classic playoff, followed by a thorough look at the Tradition scores. Then he perused the NBA roundup.

At one juncture he folded down the corner of the sports section to peer at his visitor and said, "Can you believe the Lakers? I don't see how anyone is going to beat the Lakers."

Nicklaus is a huge NBA fan—and knowledgeable. The Lakers went on to win the title.

Before moving to more serious sections of the paper, he checked out the weather...in Georgia. Cool with a chance of rain in Atlanta for the next several days. Augusta, two hours southeast, would have an identical outlook. It was hardly the optimal forecast in Nicklaus' estimation.

"I want it to be dry and fast. I always prefer that," he said. "It's the best thing for me because I'll be able to squirrel it around and hit a bunch of different shots and the other guys will try to make a score hitting it high in there and trying to stop it. I'll be able to hang in there a bit better."

The phone rang. Jackie was checking in, and Jack reviewed the final round in Scottsdale. They made plans to meet for lunch with Steve. Before Nicklaus left the house, he called Billy Morris to let him know the weather might delay his arrival into Augusta Tuesday morning, when the unveiling of a bronze statue in his honor was to occur downtown at the Georgia Golf Hall of Fame. The sculpture depicts Nicklaus holding his putter high overhead as he watches his birdie putt drop on the 17th hole in the 1986 Masters.

It turned out that the weather held off and he arrived around 10 a.m. Tuesday at Augusta's Bush Field Airport. At the ceremony

Nicklaus told the assembled thousands how important his family is to him and that the folks at Augusta, "are like an extended family to me."

⌒

The Nicklaus' primary residence in North Palm Beach (they also have their home in Muirfield Village, Ohio) is spacious, yet intimate and immaculate. Though the five children have vacated, there is no hint of an empty nest atmosphere. It is filled with the things that have made up their lives, but the living collage is a home for people and not a shrine to golf. Family pictures adorn every room. The game room walls are decorated with big catches and animal busts reflecting Jack's passion for fishing and hunting. The dining room is bursting with candleholders, which Barbara has collected from around the world.

Among the pieces of art on the walls is a small stencil drawing of a house. It was Jack and Barbara's first home in Upper Arlington, at 1845 Elmwood Ave., a two-bedroom Cape Cod style dwelling they purchased for $18,000. To Barbara it was heaven, simply because it was the first home in which she had a second bathroom. Jack's father gave the couple $1,000 as a wedding present for the down payment. Such quaint treasures answer any questions about how the Nicklauses have stayed so grounded—so normal—through the years.

In the den only three golf trophies are conspicuous: the Putter Boy trophy from his win in the 1959 North and South Amateur at Pinehurst rests on the fireplace mantle; the 1977 Memorial Tournament trophy is on the coffee table; and on a small table sits a sterling silver replica of the Augusta National clubhouse, which lists Nicklaus' six Masters wins.

There is one other prominent reminder of golf, but she freely roams the house. It's the Nicklaus' dog, Cali, a golden retriever so named because she comes from California. When prompted, she will bark six times. All Jack or Barbara has to do is ask her how many times her master has won the Masters.

Two glass trophy cases built into a hallway left of the front foyer are overflowing, as one might expect, though many mementos represent honors bestowed upon Nicklaus rather than trophies won. These honors are equally important to Nicklaus, yet they do not induce equal sentiment. He is more emotional about the former.

"I can't walk up and accept an award and treat it with a flip. I can't do that," he said. "I don't know why I get so emotional about those things, and I wish I wouldn't, but a lot of people over the years make those things happen and have supported me, and I appreciate that and get emotional over it.

"Winning a golf tournament is something else. That's different. No one is honoring me. You have to go out and do that yourself. I get emotional but in an entirely different way. It's a sense of accomplishment and there's nothing else like it."

That explains a great deal. When it came to the major championships Nicklaus was a man never more focused and also never more hungry. That was his high.

Nothing got him higher than a trip to Augusta, Georgia. To Nicklaus it is an enchanted place. As Augustans are his extended family, the National is his second home. It is no small coincidence that many facets of his Memorial Tournament emulate the Masters model.

For whatever reason, and Nicklaus is at a loss to explain it, Augusta National has always amplified his golfing self. The annual transformation occurs when Nicklaus covers the quaint 330 yards beneath the stately trees of Magnolia Lane.

They were called the Big Three in the 1960s when they lorded over golf. But as their games diminished with age, their names only continued to grow in stature. So there were Jack Nicklaus, Arnold Palmer, and Gary Player preparing to tee off together in the first round of the Masters and the world of golf still was revolving around them. Nicklaus, though, tried to remain focused on the task ahead, playing to win.

Twenty minutes before the three legends were to tee off at 1:23 p.m. the traffic areas around the first tee had become the L.A. freeway.

People stood eight to 10 deep, some perhaps because they simply could not move. Never before had the immense oak tree that stands sentinel behind the Augusta National clubhouse witnessed such a convergence of Birkenstocks, Nikes, and Dr. Scholl's. When the trio made their way from the practice green to the tee, the applause was so loud and long that it seemed a compilation sound track of ovation reaching all the way back to their glory days.

From 1958-66, the Big Three won eight of nine Masters titles and together they owned 13. But the last of them had come with Nicklaus' monumental '86 conquest. This was a largely ceremonial pairing and a special one because the three men, with a combined 130 Masters appearances covering 438 rounds, had never played together at Augusta. A larger than usual field of 95 forced the use of threesomes, making the pairing possible.

"It's a natural. It's our Millennium Match," said Phil Harrison, pairings committee chairman.

Nicklaus viewed it with mixed emotions. On Wednesday he told a press gathering, "My time at playing Augusta National has long passed. I'm here to have fun."

But he also was there to compete, and the Millennium Match lit a fuse in him. "They wouldn't have paired the three of us together if they thought any of us had a chance," he reasoned. "But I'm a funny duck, I suppose. I come here to play golf."

When he stepped on the driving range Thursday amid bright sunshine and swirling westerly winds, two desultory days of practice drifted away. A mysterious calm and confidence came over him. He started striking the ball better. Much better, more like he had in Arizona. It's often difficult to carry a good swing from the range to the course, but Nicklaus was honed in.

"Fore please, Jack Nicklaus," the announcer crowed at the appointed time, and Nicklaus, with the honor, ripped a drive down the left center of the fairway.

Palmer and Player also seemed to derive extra resources from their shared company, and through four holes all three men were even par. The first slip came at the difficult par-4 fifth, the hole Nicklaus somehow eagled twice in 1995. Palmer and Player bogeyed and the King also bogeyed the sixth and eighth. Player added another bogey at No. 9. By the 14th they each were three over par and mixing in too many wayward shots.

But Nicklaus remained level par. In fact, he made par at every hole through 15, which was good news and bad news. Par would turn out to be a handsome round on a day when the tricky winds sent the field scoring average soaring to 75.589 and allowed only nine players to break par. But Nicklaus felt he should have made it 10 after letting a bushel full of birdies escape his grasp. At No. 6, he missed from 15 feet and thus started a tidal wave of tedious endeavor. At No. 8, a three-foot tickler refused to fall. Then came errant tries from 15 feet at nine, from 10 feet at 12 after a smart 7-iron, and from 18 feet at 13.

With each miss his grimace became more pronounced, but the passion of the Golden Bear's pleas was irrelevant. The putts simply would not drop. When he missed yet another birdie try from four feet at the 15th he appeared ready to implode, his face crimson beneath his navy blue cap.

"You can only take so many shots to the ribs," he would reflect later.

Doubled over from 15, Nicklaus, or anyone else, could hardly have been shocked by the three putts lurking at 16 and 17. At 18, as to not break up the monotony, he two-putted from 25 feet for par. He signed for a disgusting 74. Player ended up with 76 and Palmer 78, and carded the only birdie.

Typical golfers, not one was happy with his score. The day was most emotional for Palmer, playing in his first Masters in 45 years without Winnie. The rapturous reception at each hole eased some of the burden.

"The crowd was very appreciative of what was happening out there," Palmer said. "I think everybody enjoyed it except maybe Gary, Jack, and myself. I didn't like my score, but I didn't play too badly either." He added, "I'll always remember this as a big part of what I've done in my career."

"Memories are the cushions of life, as they say, and playing with them was a very special experience for me," Player added. "The way people received us, that's something you appreciate because time goes by very, very quickly."

Even Nicklaus, who emphatically says he is not much for nostalgia, called the day a favorite with his old friends, "because of the significance of this place and what the three of us have accomplished here."

But he hoped to accomplish so much more in the first round, the proof of which came when Nicklaus delayed joining Palmer and Player in a post-round interview session so he could get in some work on the putting green and the practice range.

"It was the best round of golf I've played here in quite a few years, and I got absolutely nothing out of it," Nicklaus lamented as he stood tied for 32nd place and six behind the leader, Masters rookie Dennis Paulson, whose mind obviously was not cluttered by memories.

When someone pointed out to the Bear that he had beaten Tiger Woods by a shot, he could only laugh facetiously. "I didn't score what I wanted, though," was his defiant retort.

Nearly two hours later, the thought made him even angrier. "I'm trying to beat the field, not just Tiger Woods," he seethed.

There was one consolation to the day and Jackie highlighted it. As the two walked off the 18th green, son turned to father and said, "Remember what you shot the first round in '86?"

"Yeah, the same score," Jack said.

"You didn't make any putts then either," Jackie replied. "You started to make putts each day after that."

⌐

It's true about ghosts: they can go wherever they want.

They hover all around the pristine confines of Augusta National Golf Club, rub their backs on the palatial pines and occasionally, it seems, twirl their fingers over the golf balls of their favorites while dancing on the perfect emerald carpets.

Could Nicklaus see them, hear their invisible footsteps, sense their intervention?

On the ninth green Friday, just as the noon hour passed, he sighed, smiled and pointed skyward as he ambled to the cup to pluck out his third birdie of the day. What was that if not an acknowledgment of some higher force?

That putt, 35 feet above the hole, was destined for oblivion. Nicklaus had stroked his Maxfli ball much too hard, and as it curled downhill through the double break, he knew it easily could scurry off the green. The hole got in the way. The ball popped up off the back lip, and after hanging in suspended animation for a split second, plopped in.

A higher force? Or is Jack Nicklaus simply a higher force once the Masters commences?

"He walks in the place and suddenly he's 30 years old again," CBS veteran broadcaster Ken Venturi marveled. "Every year it's the same thing, an amazing transformation."

"This tournament seems to do something to pump me up. It lifts me," Nicklaus conceded. "I wish I could play one of these every week. I believe in myself when I play here."

As the second round wore on, Nicklaus, the No. 1 golfer of all time but ranked 769th in the Official World Golf Rankings, not only had himself believing, but also thousands of patrons and millions of viewers around the world. Bounding off the ninth green and shaking off the vestiges of nostalgia from a second day with his pals Palmer and Player, Nicklaus had climbed within two shots of the lead. Two strokes! Goodness how the ground shook through the old nursery. How the goose bumps swelled. Ether wafted from the dogwoods and azaleas, and euphoria gripped the masses. The gallery swelled through each new roar on the front nine.

The knowing chills of possibility started to form early, after a 2-iron stinger from 204 into the breeze at the par-3 fourth hole settled two feet from the flagstick. It was a putt Nicklaus could not miss for his first birdie. A 9-iron to eight feet set up a second one at the seventh. Nicklaus was out in 33 and stood 1 under par for the championship. But he knew he would have to maintain the pace. In the group behind, David Duval was making amends for an opening 73 by compiling five birdies and an eagle on the way to a tournament-low 65. His 138 total nosed him ahead of Phil Mickelson, Vijay Singh and Ernie Els by one stroke.

But even the stoic Duval, casting a hypnotic stare on his first green jacket, was getting caught up in the latest Nicklaus saga. "Watching him and the way everyone was going nuts, it was a neat place to be," he said.

More than that, it was intoxicating. It was inspiring. New echoes awoke dormant ones.

Golden Bear's director of communications, Scott Tolley, later that evening checked out the company web site, *Nicklaus.com*, to find it flooded with hundreds of e-mails. "We all watch you, unbelieving," wrote one fan. "How can this be possible? All my aches and pains are suddenly gone, the world is screaming JACK."

Only his unresponsive putter was impervious to the global buzz. Two rolls were required at the 10th after a 4-iron to 25 feet. Then two more putts from 18 feet at 11.

At the 12th, one of the most beguiling holes in championship golf, the Golden Bear watched with incredulity as his 7-iron cleared the front bunker but spun back in. He was forced to splash out away from the hole and his attempt for par from 14 feet was wide right. Bogey.

But he crushed a drive at 13, leaving himself 175 yards to the hole. A 5-iron set up a 20-footer for eagle. Two more putts. And so it went. Nicklaus hit 15 greens in regulation but just couldn't capitalize. Six-foot birdie putts slid by at 14 and 15.

He escaped trouble at 16 with a bunker shot to three feet. As he tromped to the 17th tee, he passed the commemorative bronze plaque affixed to a drinking fountain that was dedicated in his honor in '98. Masters officials left room at the bottom to add one more line. Was it on its way back to the engraver?

Nicklaus' monster tee shot suggested it could be. It bisected the fairway and exhausted itself 293 yards away. His 9-iron second shot left him a 15-footer that refused to drop. Another terrific drive at 18 and a 9-iron over the crest of the green appeared to give him one more great chance, but the ball spun off and backed up 30 yards. Nicklaus pitched eight feet by the hole, but his putter remained defiant, and he closed with his second bogey.

Yet as disappointing a finish as it was, there was no denying that what had transpired over the previous five-plus hours was phenomenal stuff. Forget about the new setup. With a 2-under-par 70, Nicklaus became the first player 60 or older to break par since Sam Snead's 71 a quarter century earlier. Nicklaus was level par 144 and very much in the golf tournament. Most intriguing was the collective faith among the players that he could continue this run for the ages, this run against Old Man Time and Old Man Par—the savage twin specters of golf.

"I think he can beat anybody right now," Jeff Sluman said. "Any time you underestimate an opponent, that's a terrible thing to do, and you can never underestimate Jack Nicklaus."

"On this course, how can you not consider him a serious contender?" inquired Loren Roberts.

Former British Open champ Tom Lehman used words like "remarkable" and "spectacular" to describe Nicklaus' performance. "Besides the talent of the man, it shows he knows how to play this golf course. With the success he's had he's learned something that very few people have learned."

"Was I surprised by what he'd done? Truthfully, I thought he was a bit unlucky," Player would later say.

Nicklaus would not have disagreed. Forget about being one of 57 players to make the cut. Characteristic of all golfers is the what-if reflex and Nicklaus couldn't suppress the urge, couldn't hide his disdain for what he ultimately checked off on the scorecard even as he proclaimed, "The whole day was a highlight."

"You sound like you think you should be leading," someone suggested when he had finished reeling off the litany of lost opportunities. "I don't know whether I should be leading, but I've played a lot better than my score is," Nicklaus maintained.

A very big fish had gotten away from the Bear. "Seventy is a fine score," he said later, "but it was more disappointing than the 74. It used to be I'd have gotten more out of the round than that."

Still, with 36 holes remaining Nicklaus was right where he wanted to be, more or less, and right where it seems he always is. Tied for 18th, he resided among the top 20 in the field at the midway point for the

29th time. Twenty-one times in the past he improved his position after the third round and 17 times he was among the top 10.

"My goal," he revealed, "has always been to get here and do this. That's what I've done all my life. I prepare in the spring to play for the Masters." His preparation for 2000 and the majors finally appeared to be paying off.

He seemed to be copying the script expertly from 1986, when he couldn't make a putt, shot 74-71 and found himself in 17th place before jumping to ninth after the third round and, of course, taking that historic leap to victory with a final-round 65.

White rabbits, higher forces, UFOs, 60-year-old Masters champions.

In the springtime of 2000, Jack Nicklaus made almost anything seem plausible.

⌐

You could imagine the awards ceremony Sunday. The clubhouse veranda of Augusta National drenched in sunshine. Nicklaus, smartly dressed in a gold shirt, waving to 50,000 disbelieving fans, that had just watched alchemy come to life. Barbara and the kids awash in joyful tears. CBS executives swooning over the 22 Nielsen rating and 60 share. Then the big moment, when Jose Maria Olazabal slips the green jacket over Nicklaus' shoulders—the first time the Bear enjoys the ritual with his own blazer.

Hey, whoa, you're thinking. *What's with that bit about the jacket?* Nicklaus received his in 1963, right? No. Among the hundreds of fascinating tales to emanate from the mythical grounds of Augusta National Golf Club, this is one of the most astounding.

Until 1998—35 years after he won the first of his record six green jackets—Nicklaus never owned one of the prized emerald garments made for the club by Cincinnati-based Hamilton Tailoring Co. When Nicklaus won his first Masters by one stroke over the late Tony Lema, the defending champion, Palmer, slipped a cautiously large green jacket over the hefty frame of the then 23-year-old Nicklaus. The size was a 46 long.

Jack Nicklaus acknowledges the gallery at the 18th hole at Valhalla Golf Club after completing his second round of the PGA Championship.

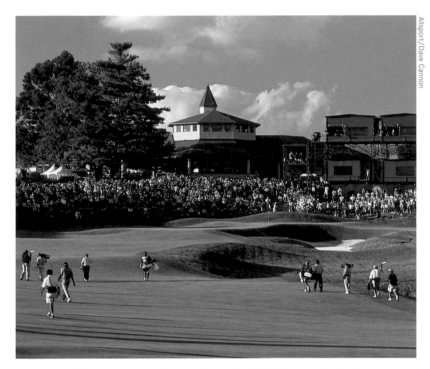

Nicklaus takes that final walk up the 18th fairway at Valhalla.

That one goes in. Nicklaus stares down an early
birdie during the second round of the PGA.

The once and future kings exchange a handshake at Valhalla.

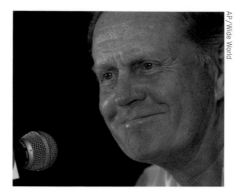

Patient as always, Jack Nicklaus meets with
the media following his second round at the PGA

Nicklaus applies another Band-Aid to his troubled right foot.

The Big Three of golf—Nicklaus, Arnold Palmer, and Gary Player—share a laugh before their opening round of the Masters at Augusta National Golf Club.

The Bear and his son, Jackie, size up a putt at the Masters.

The two old foes, Nicklaus and Palmer, share a walk up the fairway
at Augusta as Palmer acknowledges cheers from the gallery.

Jack and Barbara Nicklaus share a light moment with two grandchildren at the Memorial Tournament Honoree ceremonies at Muirfield Village Golf Club.

Nicklaus fights his emotions as he speaks to the crowd at Muirfield Village.

Nicklaus gazes out at the Pacific Ocean on the 18th tee at Pebble Beach
Golf Links before playing his final hole at the 100th U.S. Open.

Jack lets it rip with his tee shot at Pebble's 18th hole.

Nicklaus, with help from Jackie, dabs away tears
after reaching Pebble's 18th green.

After leaving his eagle putt at the 18th hole short,
Nicklaus playfully turns his cap sideways.

Jack tips his hat to the crowd at the 18th hole at Pebble Beach.

Barbara greets Jack with a kiss behind the 18th green
at Pebble Beach when it was all over.

Jack Nicklaus launches a drive at the 18th hole at the
Old Course in St. Andrews, Scotland, during the British Open.

Nicklaus waits to putt out on the final hole, with the
Royal & Ancient clubhouse looming nearby.

Standing on the Swilken Burn Bridge, Jack Nicklaus waves
goodbye to the Scottish fans at St. Andrews.

"It was like an overcoat," Nicklaus recalled. "It just hung on me. It was huge."

The jacket was merely for show at the awards presentation. Nicklaus hid its oversized proportions well, never straightening his arms during the ceremony. Club officials promised to have a jacket made for their newest honorary member, but when he returned in '64 he found no authentic three-buttoned, single-vented blazer awaiting him. Unperturbed, he borrowed a jacket from Thomas Dewey, the former governor of New York—the man of "Dewey Beats Truman" fame who nearly won the 1948 presidential election.

In the early 1970s, after having won his record-tying fourth Masters title, Nicklaus still did not own a green jacket and Dewey's was becoming bedraggled. Nicklaus decided to have one made for him by clothier Hart, Schaffner and Marx.

"It was not even the same material or really the right color," said Nicklaus, who could not care less since he is red-green colorblind.

Nicklaus won a record fifth green jacket in 1975 in dramatic fashion, but by the end of the decade his copycat coat was in need of replacement. Again he went the route of borrower and went through a series of other members' jackets. Even after his phenomenal '86 triumph the Golden Bear still was on the take, but by now he was quietly relishing the irony. He told no one at the club about this until 1997 when he chided club chairman Jack Stephens. "You know, I've won this tournament six times and I've never been given a green jacket."

Stephens was stunned. He ordered Nicklaus into the clubhouse immediately for a fitting, but Nicklaus, incorrigibly mischievous, couldn't be swayed.

"It's such a great story I don't want to ruin it," he told Stephens.

But the chairman's decision rules at Augusta. When Nicklaus returned in 1998, the year of the plaque dedication in his honor, he found a note from Stephens in his locker. A jacket fitting was scheduled. No exceptions. No excuses. That week, 40 years after making his first visit to Augusta National, Jack Nicklaus proudly donned his very own green jacket—size 44 regular.

⌒

Saturday is called moving day in golf, and when Nicklaus, fresh from 10 hours of sleep, emerged from his rented house in the Conifer Place subdivision a couple of miles from the club, he sensed a day of low scores. Skies were overcast, but it was warm with only a hint of a breeze. He was nervous, a good sign. It had been two years since he last was in the hunt for a major title. He felt up to the challenge.

"I never get pumped up about golf, but I was ready to go play," he said. "I was ready to chase after it and see how good I could still chase."

Unfortunately, he was delayed out of the starting blocks. The skies began to darken around lunch time and play was suspended at 12:25 p.m., just as Nicklaus and Ian Woosnam, the diminutive Welshman who won the '91 Masters, were preparing to tee off. By the time play resumed at 2:30, there was a lingering rain but the wind had subsided. Conditions were rather benign.

Nicklaus bogeyed the third hole with a three-putt but immediately answered by birdieing the tough fourth for the second straight day. Another three-putt at the sixth pushed him back into green figures. He didn't know it at the time, but those six holes were his window of opportunity. The sun broke through at about 4 p.m. But within a half-hour, the temperature inexplicably plummeted from the low 70s to the mid-50s. Then the northwest winds began to gust to 20, 30, and as high as 42 miles per hour.

Nicklaus later said, "I've never seen a tougher day at Augusta."

Few days there ever have been as weird. "It was a lottery on every shot," Sluman said.

The gusting wind moved pinecones, caps, leaves, green sandwich wrappers, unattended folding chairs and clumps of pine straw. And golf balls, too. Nick Faldo intentionally missed the green with a wedge at the 17th and watched his ball get redirected to within four feet of the cup. There were similar tales all over the storied course.

Tree branches were embedded, some sticking upright, in the manicured grass. A golf ball nearly embedded itself on the 12th green. Nothing unusual about that, except that Tiger Woods was lining up a treacherous downhill chip from behind the green with his golf ball resting on pine straw when another ball dropped out of the sky and stopped 20 feet to his left.

It had come from adjacent Augusta Country Club behind the 12th hole. Not surprisingly, no one claimed the wayward shot.

"You know that scene from Caddyshack II, where the ball just went up over the fence?" said Woods. "It was just splat, all over the green."

Scoring went splat, too. A mere five players among the 49 who completed their round broke par, and they were early finishers. Only Singh, playing in the final group with Duval, would shoot under par among those who completed their third round early Sunday—a remarkable performance.

Nicklaus was holding it together in the increasingly faster and harder conditions, going out in a creditable 37. As he trudged up the slope from the ninth green to the 10th tee, he turned to Woosnam and said, "If we play a decent back nine we'll be right in the middle of this thing."

But April, already the cruelest month, was about to turn crueler still. Immediately Nicklaus gave away another shot at the long, downhill par-4 10th. He cut a 4-wood "pretty as can be," he said, into the recontoured green and watched stupefied as the ball skidded off the putting surface and under a bush. A good chip left him a 10-foot par putt that went awry. It was the type of putt you could almost count on him nailing in his heyday.

At 11, the porthole to the famed Amen Corner, another shot almost slipped away, but he got one to go down from 20 feet for par. Nicklaus was struggling, but he was far from out of the golf tournament. He needed to hang on, dig in, and keep converting pars; in short, do the things he had done so well for so many years. As Johnny Miller once said, no one ever understood the value of par better than Jack Nicklaus. The conditions, though unpleasant, seemed to turn the competition in his favor.

But now he had to negotiate the deceptive par-3 12th hole. Golden Bell, as the hole is named, is 155 yards and protected in front by Rae's Creek and a deep bunker. The elevated green also is harrowingly shallow. Behind lurks another bunker, then a steep, foliage-covered rise and tall pine trees. The pines nearly obscure the view of Augusta CC, but more acutely they disguise the wind swirling through Amen Corner, the lowest part of the course. Proper club selection requires almost divine intervention.

Nicklaus' most memorable shot at the 12th hole occurred in 1964 when he shanked an 8-iron and watched in horror as the ball whistled over the heads of Bob Jones and Clifford Roberts seated in a nearby golf cart. In 1963, when he won his first Masters, and in 1986, when he shot 30 on the back nine on the way to that improbable sixth green jacket, the Bear bogeyed No. 12.

On this turbulent afternoon, Nicklaus chose a 6-iron, a club he rarely pulls there. His standard play is to aim a 7-iron directly over the front bunker. Sure enough, the 6-iron was too much. The ball bore through the wind and carried into the back bunker. When he arrived there, a poor position looked even worse. The ball had nestled between rake furrows, which meant he would be unable to put any spin on the shot. Catch it too clean and he risked rinsing it in Rae's Creek. Too fat and par was unlikely. Compounding it all is that Nicklaus is uneasy in the heavy silica that fills Augusta's bunkers. It was an intimidating shot for anyone.

Playing conservatively, as is his inclination, Nicklaus aimed away from the hole and tried to hit down more firmly to prevent blasting it into Rae's Creek. But he got too tentative and left it in. Now he'd have to fight for bogey. But the next explosion wasn't much better, and he barely scraped it out. Putting from the fringe, Nicklaus left his bogey attempt short. Shockingly, the three-footer for a five also stayed up. He tapped in. Six. Triple bogey. He was stunned. He was stung. Only three other times in all his Masters visits had he played a hole in more than two over par.

"I figured, 'There goes the golf tournament,'" Nicklaus said.

But he quickly regrouped. He admonished himself quietly for the defeatism that had crept into his consciousness. "I told myself that was a ridiculous attitude," he said. "A good birdie here could erase some of the mistakes at 12 and I could stay close. I hit one of my best drives of the year at 13."

That left him 166 yards to the front of the green and 199 to the hole. He chose a 3-iron and struck a low draw off the sidehill lie. Halfway there he was thinking eagle. "It was about as good as I could hit it," he said. "I thought it would get next to the hole." But the wind had other ideas. It stood the ball up and knocked the shot into the creek. Nicklaus did well to make a six out of it. But another shot was lost.

What commenced was a series of good shots and grotesque results and he couldn't stop losing strokes. The wind chilled him and the hard greens had become a mystery he couldn't solve, and he was trapped in the jaws of a savage golf course. He bogeyed three of the final five holes, completing a back-nine 44 and a 9-over 81. It was his highest Masters score and the first time in 155 rounds that Nicklaus had failed to break 80.

History had been changed.

In the aftermath Nicklaus was in surprisingly good humor, considering how quickly his chances for one last run had ended. "This isn't Memorial weather. We'd love this," he joked, referring to the cycle of poor conditions that have plagued his tournament.

"I felt like I was playing golf with a ball-peen hammer and a marble on a marble floor," he quipped.

But there was pain beneath the punch lines. It was there when he assessed his play with his usual candor. "These conditions are tough on me," he admitted. "I'm not as good in them as I used to be. I've never been a great wind player, but I'd have handled them better years ago. I played myself out of it."

He hid the disappointment well. As he turned to leave the assemblage of reporters, Nicklaus sought out his son. "C'mon, let's go hit a few hundred balls."

⤳

With no chase in him—and nothing to chase after—Nicklaus submitted a perfunctory 6-over 78 in the final round while playing with reigning U.S. Amateur champion David Gossett.

"I'm going to have a hard time getting up to play," he had told Barbara Sunday morning over breakfast.

Sure enough, Nicklaus gave a genuine effort, but the energy was lacking when he and Gossett embarked at 10:15 a.m. "I tried to play as best I could, but I just couldn't get much enthusiasm going," he said after finishing in a tie for 54th place at 15-over 303. He did not convert a birdie and he seldom gave himself a realistic chance at one. He bogeyed the final three holes, one fewer than the number of birdies he recorded for the week.

But in that cold, crisp morning air, Nicklaus found himself enveloped in the warm embrace of the multitudes eager to pay him homage. Nicklaus truly appreciates the sincere applause and the people who shower it upon him. How can he not be touched? But on another, more practical level, he despises its implicit nod to the past.

· "It's all very nice, but I want them to recognize me for what I'm doing and not what I've done years ago," he said.

Problem is, what Nicklaus did in the past no longer bears on the present—at least as it relates to touring the golf course. For Nicklaus, the most significant event of a pleasant spring day that ended in Vijay Singh's first Masters triumph was one last regretful discovery that history—his history anyway—had been wiped clean. "I had at least six putts today that I knew from memory, last day pin placements, and they went in the opposite direction," Nicklaus explained. "That surprised me. Memory is not of any asset now."

That was true on the golf course, and in many other places. So much for the cushions of life.

"It just wasn't the same," he said of his return. "All in all I enjoyed the golf tournament. I thought the golf course was pretty good. You were rewarded for good shots. But it was not the same atmosphere, not the same course. Not the same."

No wonder he couldn't say—he refused to say—that he would be back. "It's possible that was my last walk at 18. I'm not saying it was, I'm not saying it wasn't."

It took less than 10 minutes for Nicklaus to visit the champions' locker room, change shoes, and exit the clubhouse.

"Where did I go wrong?" he asked Jackie as he left, bewilderment predominant in his tone. "Gosh, I played my way off into the sunset."

He got in his forest green Lincoln Town Car with his son and Pandel Savic, general chairman of his Memorial Tournament. As the car eased out of the circle and toward Magnolia Lane, two patrons ran up alongside, clutching items to be signed. The car stopped, and Nicklaus rolled down the window and graciously obliged.

As the car resumed its journey, possibly for the last time with Nicklaus in tow, the couple, a man and a woman, smiled broadly as they beheld their pieces of history.

5

HOME

A MEMORIAL TO REMEMBER

Muirfield Village Golf Club, the posh and polished private club in Dublin, Ohio, that annually hosts the Memorial Tournament on the PGA Tour, is the embodiment not so much of golfing opulence but of all the redeeming qualities instilled in a son by his doting and diligent father.

As much as his 20 major tournament victories, Muirfield Village— named after Muirfield, the course of the Honourable Company of Edinburgh Golfers in Scotland, where Nicklaus first played abroad in the 1959 Walker Cup, then won his first British Open in '66—stands as an appropriate representation of the life and values of Jack Nicklaus. It is a life he never would have known if not for his benevolent father, Charlie, who introduced him to the game, supported him unwaveringly as he pursued it with passion, and expected from him a level of accomplishment—in all pursuits—that exceeded the accepted norms. This being the case, there are few things of this earth that mean more to Nicklaus than Muirfield Village and the Memorial, a tournament that has fulfilled successfully the dual mission intended by its founder: stage a golf event that is a first-rate experience for both players and fans; celebrate the game by honoring figures who have contributed to its growth. Nicklaus considers the tournament one of his greatest accomplishments.

The 25th Memorial Tournament stood to be one of the most momentous occasions of Nicklaus' career for the singular reason that he was the 2000 Honoree. Nicklaus had mixed emotions about being the 30th individual to be enshrined in Memorial Park. He was deeply moved, but he expected—and would have preferred—that it occur later in his life. When Payne Stewart died on October 25, 1999 in a Learjet crash, Nicklaus offered to make way for Stewart to be honored in 2000, but the Captains Club, which advises the tournament's executive committee on pertinent tournament business and selects the Honoree, was intractable on the issue. It had decided five years ago for the millennial orchestration of ceremonies for Nicklaus, and it wasn't about to alter that plan—even for Stewart.

"I created the animal and now it has come back to me," Nicklaus said with a nervous chuckle. The very thought of the ceremonies made him uneasy, and his apprehension had grown each day since he heard the news during the 1999 Memorial.

The timing of such an emotional event couldn't have come at a worse time for his golf game. The Memorial was his last event before the U.S. Open, he wasn't coming in particularly sharp, and the emotional burden of accepting the award and delivering a speech would place golf on a farther backburner than usual. Nicklaus seldom has been able to give his golf game the proper attention during tournament week anyway, so wrapped up has he been in every detail of its operation. It's a chore to post a score when you're preoccupied with picking up cigarette butts and stuffing them in your caddie's pocket, as Nicklaus often did in the tournament's early years. Once he summoned one of his minions to the tee in the middle of a round to discuss the merits of green wrapping paper for the concession sandwiches.

Even today Nicklaus takes nurturing to new levels, like his practice of dousing his divots with bottled water.

Nicklaus estimates that for years he spotted the field two shots per round, which is why he classifies the first of his two Memorial victories in 1977 (he also won in '84) the most difficult and rewarding of his career—surpassing even his '86 Masters triumph. That first win on his home course—delayed by rain until Monday, of course—was monumental because it had come at home, on his own creation, and because he was so little prepared for competition due to the suffocating array of host duties dominating his time in the tournament's early years.

"I've poured most of my life for the last 35 years into what's happened in this golf tournament and...the golf course and everything else. It's been a fairly emotional thing for me. I can't think of anything else that I've been more involved in more completely other than my family and my playing golf than Muirfield Village."

Again, none of this would have come to fruition if not for his father and the famous ankle injury. Charlie Nicklaus injured his ankle playing recreational volleyball in 1944, but five years later, when he began to have trouble with it, doctors found he had actually chipped a bone. To correct the problem, the ankle joint had to be fused. His doctor, Jud Wilson, recommended walking as a means of rehabilitation. Charlie decided golf would be the most enjoyable form of pedestrian recreation and enlisted his 10-year-old son as companion and caddie. Those good walks spoiled nothing but young Jackie's future ambitions in other avenues. With the fortuitous arrival of Jack Grout, Nicklaus soon immersed himself wholly in all aspects of the game and embarked on a golfing life unlike any other.

Charlie Nicklaus never saw Muirfield Village, which is the flagship golf course among the nearly 200 Jack has designed. But his influence is everywhere, delivered through Jack's vision of how details, large and small, ought to be presented.

"I think my father would have loved Muirfield," said Nicklaus, who as a youngster used to hunt with his dad on the ground, abounding in woods, where the course now sits. "He would have loved it. He pushed me to do it. He knew what I wanted to do. He was the one who kept encouraging me. That is one of the biggest things I have missed about my father; he understood me. He understood how I think. I miss that connection with him."

Muirfield, spread out over 240 rolling acres produced by glacial intervention, might not have happened without the elder Nicklaus' conspicuous support. Mark McCormack of International Management Group in Cleveland was managing Nicklaus' business affairs at the time when Nicklaus was personally financing the land acquisitions for the course. He did not endorse the plan and fretted over the stress, financial and otherwise, it was inflicting on his client.

"McCormack was having a heart attack that I was doing Muirfield," Nicklaus recalled.

"Why are you doing this?" McCormack would ask.

Nicklaus, young and brash, would respond blithely, "Because I want to."

"But it's costing you all your money."

"I don't care. This is what I want to do."

It nearly ruined him financially. "Muirfield did cost me a little. It almost cost me a lot," he admitted. "But I decided that's what my contribution should be to golf. My dad certainly would have approved of what it became."

His father would have approved because Muirfield Village became such a profound statement of excellence along the lines of Augusta National Golf Club. The comparison is not coincidental.

Bobby Jones and Nicklaus founded their respective clubs with the best intentions and the highest ideals. Their success was largely predicated on the respect they engendered not only as unquestioned champions of their respective eras, but also as pillars of sportsmanship. Each man had a codesigning role (Jones with Alister MacKenzie, Nicklaus with Desmond Muirhead) in golf courses that reflect similar philosophies. Augusta and Muirfield are second-shot golf courses, though Muirfield, with its heavily bunkered, elevated greens is much more of a modern aerial test. Each course is ranked among the best in America.

The idea of building a golf course and bringing a PGA Tour event to his Columbus, Ohio, hometown even took root during the 1966 Masters, though ideas were percolating a year or two earlier when Nicklaus engaged Paul Hornung, the sports editor of the *Columbus Dispatch*, in conversations about the absence of a tour event and what could be done to alter those circumstances. Nicklaus would have been all of 24 at the time. On Wednesday, November 13, 1974, the *Dispatch* reported a major golf tournament would be held at Muirfield Village. Not surprisingly, the *Dispatch* referred to the tournament as "The Masters of the North," after Nicklaus said his tournament would draw heavily in style and flavor from the Masters. Nicklaus solicited advice from persnickety Clifford Roberts, the longtime chairman of Augusta and the mastermind of the Masters. Roberts agreed to serve on the Captains Club.

Nicklaus' ambition for the event was direct and simple, and was expressed long before the first Memorial round on May 27, 1976. "You might say it will be a showplace…what tournament golf should be, a way for me to best relate what I think great golf and great tournaments should be."

It's been one of the best shows on the PGA Tour, ever since Roger Maltbie defeated Hale Irwin in the inaugural tournament with the help of an approach shot that fortuitously caromed off a gallery stake. Twelve of the 20 champions have won major championships and the Memorial, with its operational attention to detail and the power of the Nicklaus name attached, traditionally ranks among the top 10 strongest fields despite some of the consistently worst weather of any venue.

Additionally, Muirfield Village, the first of what are known as "stadium courses," with planned spectator areas, has welcomed other marquee events. Since it opened in 1974, it has hosted the 1987 Ryder Cup—site of the Europeans' first victory on American soil—the '92 U.S. Amateur, won by Justin Leonard, and the '98 Solheim Cup, the women's biennial match play competition.

The show came to a complete halt at 3 p.m. Wednesday, May 24, as the legendary composure of the Golden Bear was put to the ultimate test in a moving 50-minute ceremony.

With the exception of the absence of the two men who most impacted his life and career—his father and his teacher, Jack Grout—Nicklaus enjoyed a perfect afternoon. The sun emerged overhead for a change. An estimated 20,000 people, including Barbara, their children and grandchildren, his sister, Marilyn Hutchinson, and his 90-year-old mother, Helen, surrounded the 18th green. Players usually skip the ceremony, but 40 or so gathered to the left of the podium on this occasion.

"I wanted to be there because of my respect for him not only as a player but as a person," Fuzzy Zoeller explained.

The prelude to Nicklaus' 20-minute speech was gloriously touching. PGA Tour commissioner Tim Finchem led off the tribute. Nicklaus' fellow Big Three members, Palmer and Gary Player, followed, and they delivered emotionally contrasting speeches. Palmer choked up talking of his deep friendship with Jack and Barbara, a friendship that had grown deeper after the death of Palmer's wife, Winnie. Player called Nicklaus, "a man for all seasons," but sifted in a few quips with the compliments.

Finchem: "As great as Jack Nicklaus' competitive record on the golf course is, it is his passion for the etiquette, his professionalism that has stood out…Can you ever recall an instance when you turned from the television set or walked down the ropes of a golf tournament and said, 'I wish he hadn't said that,' or 'I wish he hadn't made that gesture?'…Jack Nicklaus has always been the epitome of what professionalism is in golf."

Palmer: "Jack has won a lot of tournaments and we know that. But do we ever think of the tournaments that he lost? And he has lost a few. And my point is, he has done both with great dignity."

Player couldn't resist a few barbs, especially about his habitual tardiness: "If he was a race horse being so late, he would have been shot." And of Nicklaus' prodigious appetite he said, "This man was no slouch with a knife and fork. If you weren't watching very carefully he'd butter your hand."

"A great football coach once said that you show me a good loser and I'll show you a non-winner," Player added. "Well, Jack Nicklaus has defied that."

What Nicklaus could not defy this day was the emotional static that blurred his vision and sent his chin quivering. Only a few times had he ever displayed such emotion, most recently at the '98 Masters. Then there was the occasion of the first Memorial, in '76, when he delivered a speech about the first Honoree, Bobby Jones, and found his voice cracking as thoughts of his dad flooded his mind.

He spoke eloquently, but he hurried through his 13-page oration, not out of nervousness, but for fear that he wouldn't be able to finish it. It was only the second speech he had ever prepared in writing (the first was in 1984 when he received an honorary doctorate from St. Andrews University in Scotland), and he had broken down as he rehearsed it on the plane en route to Ohio.

"Columbus truly represents the confluence of my personal and professional life," he began, already sniffling from an earlier purging of tears. He dabbed his eyes on several occasions and nervously put his hand to his mouth on others.

"Where we stand today is obviously a very special place to me as it pulls together so many aspects of my life," Nicklaus said, his voice cracking. "My hope is that Muirfield Village will forever stand as a representation for my love and respect of the game, and the Memorial for my passion for tournament golf."

Nicklaus stammered when talking about Jack Grout and about the pride he felt that his son, Gary, who followed in his footsteps at Ohio State, had qualified on his own merits for the tournament field. But he encountered his most difficult moments when he spoke of Barbara and of his father.

"Success is all about timing." Now he had to start pushing words out. "And never is timing more important than in the game of golf. I can say with conviction that my timing has never been better than that day in 1957, outside Mendenhall Lab on the campus of Ohio State University, when I met Barbara Jean Bash...Were it not for Barbara, I would have been just another golfer."

A few pauses later, he mentioned the ankle injury his father suffered that started Nicklaus on the path to golf greatness. "My father always loved telling that story," Nicklaus eked out, "and I'm sure that if anyone up there is willing to listen, he's still telling it.

"I was recently asked what event, golf or otherwise, would I have liked to have my father witness. I said today, because that would mean that I would have had my father for the last 30 years of my life...and he wouldn't have missed a thing."

When he had finished, he kissed Barbara and gave his mother, seated in a wheelchair, a hug. Helen Nicklaus had not been well the past few years, but she had defied the odds to witness this day, when the memories of her husband, gone 30 years, were made vivid and fresh.

"I wish Dad could have been here," Jack whispered to her.

"He was," she assured him.

All anyone had to do was look around.

⌐

From her chair to the right of her husband, Barbara Nicklaus, wearing her gray club jacket (she served as captain of the 1996 tournament) had looked on the proceedings proudly but with great pain. She had been feeling poorly for several days. Her abdomen was sore but she kept it from Jack and ingested six Advil prior to the ceremonies. She didn't want to ruin his moment, one of the most important of his life and career—a career for which she had made great sacrifices.

Sacrificing for her husband is something Barbara Nicklaus had done instinctively. She accommodated him and his needs since they met. Their respective roles in the relationship were established early. Barbara enrolled in prenursing, a work-intensive five-year course to be completed in four years. That was an untenable situation to the son of a pharmacist.

"You can't go to school in the summer because you're going to be dating me," Jack told her.

She switched to elementary education. She even took a course on golf at OSU and began to play a little. The first time she played with Jack, she bogeyed the first hole and told him, "This doesn't seem so hard. I don't understand why you practice so much."

Without a doubt, Muirfield Village is more than just Jack's dream. As she did with all things to which he devoted his energies, Barbara made it a part of her dreams, too. The end product reflects her influence as much as it does her husband's.

Pandel Savic, the tournament's general chairman, goes further, having said once, "In essence, it's Barbara's tournament. Jack sets the standard but Barbara sets the tone of how we achieve the quality."

Through the years, particularly in the tournament's infancy, Barbara compiled a list of suggested improvements for the tournament and the club. Some years the list was long. Many times the items on it were costly. Displaying the kind of stubbornness that her husband showed in getting the enterprise off the ground, Barbara eventually saw to it that everything got checked off. While Jack has devoutly tinkered with the golf course—and would do so yet again after the 2000 tournament—Barbara has obsessed over all the elements around it, from scoreboards to stairways and walkways to amenities for fans, players, and their spouses.

When Jack needed a representative to approach the Honourable Company of Edinburgh Golfers in Muirfield, Scotland, to discuss his desire to have Muirfield Village copy its club captain tradition, he selected Barbara. During her visit abroad the Honourable Company could not have been more accommodating, even inviting her into the clubhouse for a tour, an unprecedented gesture of respect from the insular all-male club.

Her respect in the golf world is universal. She has received numerous honors for her charity work and for her contributions to the game. She has raised more than $10 million for various philanthropies.

The weeks following the Masters had been active for the Nicklauses on the awards front. Jack accepted the third annual Dave Marr Memorial Award April 28 at the Shell Houston Open for his dedication to sportsmanship and golf. (Later in the year would come more honors, including the PGA of America's Distinguished Service Award and the inaugural Payne Stewart Award, which he shared with Arnold Palmer and Byron Nelson.) A week later, meanwhile, the Metropolitan Golf Writers Association named Barbara the first recipient of the Winnie Palmer Award for her consistent efforts on behalf of those less fortunate. She accepted that award June 4 in New York.

A decade earlier the World Series of Golf in Akron, Ohio, honored her as its Ambassador of Golf. Talk about sweet irony. The first golf tournament Barbara ever saw was in Akron. She accompanied Jack and his parents to Firestone Country Club for the 1958 Rubber City

Open. The three followed Jack all 18 holes. On the way home Jack, as any golfer is wont to do, began reviewing his round aloud.

"Do you remember the second shot on the 13th hole?" he asked her.

What? "I was thinking, 'I don't even remember the 13th hole, how am I going to remember the second shot?'" she recalled. "And then I thought, this is never going to work. I'm never going to be able to talk golf with him."

It didn't matter. She loved him so—still loves him so. She has talked often of how they have grown up together during his march to excellence, but their relationship retains elements of schoolyard romance. On Air Bear, the Nicklaus' private jet, they sit across from each other in plush green leather captain's chairs. She might be reading a book or magazine and to get her attention, he'll playfully kick the bottom of her foot, like some shy adolescent. She'll peer up at him and smile, elements of a teenage crush in her eyes. This is how a marriage can last for 40 years.

Nicklaus was relieved, to say the least, when the speeches had ended and the cameras from The Golf Channel—which never before had televised the Honoree ceremonies—had been switched off. He never has been much for pomp and circumstance. Having to speak in front of people from his hometown about the most personal aspects of his life had weighed heavily on his mind for a year.

Thirty-eight years ago Jack Nicklaus Day was celebrated in Columbus after his triumph in the U.S. Open. That had been a snap. "I was a kid then. You don't pay attention to what's going on."

This was different. So much different. A young Nicklaus had only the charge of possibilities surging through him. He was not weighed down by 40 more years of memories, trials, tribulations, triumphs and even a few regrets—the unavoidable baggage of sentimentality that comes with growing older. What's more, the occasion forced him to fight the current of his own inclinations, the ones that always kept him thinking forward.

"That was the most emotional situation I've probably ever been in from a golfing standpoint," he admitted. "It's just tough when you're coming in front of so many people you've known for so many years, the game that you love, and the place that you love, where you grew up …it's not easy, talking about people who haven't been here for awhile."

Nicklaus always has been more comfortable with a club in his hand and a shot to be played. He couldn't wait to get back to those kinds of challenges.

"I should breeze through the tournament," he said with a relieved smile. "It should be an easy win now."

On the contrary, there was a lot of work to be done. A lot of work.

⌒

Between the Masters and the Memorial Tournament, Nicklaus caught up on his wide array of design projects. In one stretch he covered five states in three days, including a return to Hokulia in Hawaii. He squeezed in just two tournaments. One was right on the heels of the Masters—a third straight major, and a second senior installment, the PGA Seniors' Championship April 13-16 in Palm Beach Gardens, Florida.

Nicklaus describes the par-5 second hole at Augusta National as "my least favorite hole in major championship golf." His favorites include the par-4 eighth at Pebble Beach, the par-4 17th "Road Hole" on the Old Course at St. Andrews, and the par-5 13th at Augusta. Yet perhaps the most difficult hole also comes from the Masters; it is the emotional one a player must climb out of the week afterward. There is little a player can do to avert the dreaded Masters hangover. It afflicts nearly every participant, but it is most devastating to those who finish highest on the leaderboard. It can last anywhere from a few days to a few months to even longer as Greg Norman or Tom Weiskopf can attest.

"The closer you get to winning and not doing so, the harder it gets to come back," Nicklaus said. "But it doesn't last long, just a few days."

A few days were all Nicklaus could afford. The 61st PGA Seniors' at PGA National Resort & Spa represented a third straight week of major competition, a quirk in the schedule that was going to be corrected beginning in 2001 with senior tour schedule changes.

Played on the Champion Course at PGA National, which Nicklaus redesigned in 1990, the PGA Seniors' is the oldest senior tournament. The tournament was begun in 1937 at Augusta National Golf Club and was played there two years. Nicklaus, who won his only PGA Seniors' title in 1991, the year he won three of the four senior majors and became the only player to complete the career senior slam, lives a mere 10 minutes from the course. That was a blessing considering the stretch of miserable weather—the third week running—that plagued the tournament.

Except for rookie Doug Tewell, who with a 15-under-201 total triumphed in the first 54-hole finish since 1958, it was a wholly unmemorable week. Rain and lightning plagued each of the first four days and no single round was completed in one day, forcing an elimination of one round and a Monday finish.

Nicklaus tied for 12th and pocketed $33,200 after shooting 71-71-72-214 on the 6,770-yard, par-72 layout that he classified as the most difficult on the senior tour. He played decently, with a sole highlight coming in the final round when he holed a 7-iron from 169 yards at the par-4 eighth hole for his first eagle of the year.

The tournament's most enduring moment occurred on Friday when more than four inches of rain flushed the Champion Course down to the ocean and no golf was played.

Nicklaus was holed up in the players' dining area adjacent to the pro shop and was munching on a sandwich when a frantic fan, standing outside in the rain, peered through the glass and was wildly waving his arms with a sense of urgency, trying to get the Bear's attention. Alarmed, Nicklaus headed toward the door. "I figured it had to be something important."

Oh, it was. "Jack," the man asked breathlessly, "do you know if Arnold is in there?" Nicklaus could only shake his head and laugh. As amazing as it seems, sometimes it's just not enough to be Jack Nicklaus.

A few weeks passed before Nicklaus elected to make another PGA Tour appearance, with son Gary, prior to the Memorial. He chose the Compaq Classic of New Orleans, which began May 4 at English Turn Golf and Country Club. Jack hadn't played in the tournament since 1991, when he finished 14th in what was then called the USF&G Classic. Nicklaus appeared for the 18th time in the tournament and the fourth time since it moved from Lakewood Country Club, where he won in 1973. Despite the presence of five of the top 10 players in the world rankings, the $3.4 million event received the biggest boost from the presence of the course designer, the Bear himself.

Playing with reigning Masters champion Vijay Singh, and wielding a new putter, Nicklaus opened with a promising 70 and got a boost by using that putter a mere 24 times. "This one makes putts," Nicklaus said happily, explaining the difference from other models he'd been using.

Singh was happy, too, after shooting 68. He was glad the day was over. "It's nerve-wracking playing with him," Singh said. "I mean, it's Jack Nicklaus."

Lots of weird things happen to people when Nicklaus is around. Take Mario Gallioto, one of the marshals at the Compaq Classic. As Nicklaus walked up No. 18 on Friday, Gallioto, of New Orleans, was among those applauding wildly. He then hushed the crowd, holding up a sign that said, "Quiet Please," as the Golden Bear looked over a par putt. When ducks swimming in the pond adjacent to the green began to quack loudly, Gallioto waved the sign at them and demanded quiet.

The ducks obeyed.

Nicklaus' putter, which had been so brilliant the previous day, did not obey him, however, in Round 2. He shot 77-147, two better than Gary, and missed the cut by four strokes. Worse than missing the cut, however, was the apparent backpedaling that he'd done since the Masters. In all phases he seemed to be regressing.

"The shots I wasted...that just wasn't like me," he said, the thought obviously gnawing at him. "I didn't hit it good and I didn't putt very well. I had a lot of awkward shots. That's how you shoot 77."

The warm reception from the gallery only made him angrier with himself.

"You know me. It was very nice, but I want them to give me a nice reception for the way I'm playing golf, not my record.

"Right now," he grumbled. "I'm not playing worth a darn."

⌐

One of the most often expressed criticisms of Nicklaus' golf courses is that many of his early designs he tailored to his own playing tendencies—too many dogleg right holes, too many greens receptive only to high-flying long irons. Nicklaus has refuted the theory with his performance on some of the 59 Nicklaus courses that have hosted tournaments. Of his 70 PGA Tour wins, only four came on his courses—the two Memorials, the 1973 Ohio Kings Island Open, and the 1975 Heritage Classic at Harbour Town, which he codesigned with Pete Dye. Only six times in 25 starts has he placed in the top 10 at Muirfield Village.

Sure, he has plundered Desert Mountain for four Tradition wins. His one victory on the redesigned Champion Course at PGA National was achieved despite the fact that the intimacy with which he knows the layout is a detriment to his mindset. "Maybe because I think the golf course is tougher than the other guys do," he said.

At Muirfield Village his problem is a passivity born of affection.

"I haven't played particularly well here many years. It is odd for me to say, but this is a tough golf course for me. I have a hard time playing the golf course and maybe it's because I know it so well. I'm in love with it, so it's probably more difficult for me to get tough with it."

In a windy opening round of the 25th Memorial, Nicklaus had to get tough or face missing his sixth Memorial cut and fifth in seven years. Including a double-bogey at the par-4 ninth, Nicklaus played the opening nine holes in 5-over-par 41. When he bogeyed the short par-4 14th to go six over, he grew morbidly curious. "I was thinking to myself, 'What am I going to shoot? Am I going to shoot a snowman?'"

A snowman is 80 or more, and in 84 previous rounds at Muirfield, he had failed to break 80 once.

Only a miraculous finish prevented a second Frosty. He converted an 11-foot birdie at the par-5 15th, one of three par-5 holes he had altered and lengthened, and a 172-yard 8-iron to four feet set up another birdie at the 17th. A wayward approach at the last just skirted the front left bunker and he took advantage by chipping in from 20 feet away. A 75 wouldn't usually elicit positive feelings, nor would his nine-shot deficit to leader Harrison Frazar. But on a day when the scoring average inched up to 74.352, Nicklaus knew he had pulled off a great escape.

There are few athletes today who sign more autographs than Nicklaus. This is due, in almost equal parts, to golfers' accessibility to their fans and Nicklaus' steadfast dedication to the kids and adults who genuinely want his signature for their own enjoyment.

The Nicklaus signature is highly coveted, and Nicklaus must be generous with it sometimes and protective of it at other times. He, Palmer, and Woods collectively spent nearly $2 million in legal fees in 2000 trying to fend off forgers and the misuse of their names on suspect memorabilia. In recent years, with the growth of e-Bay and other Internet auction sites, there has been an increasing proliferation of profiteering autograph seekers. The pros are easy to spot. They carry backpacks full of items. One of their most popular ploys is enlisting the help of children, giving them as little as $5 to turn on their youthful charms and acquire the autograph for them.

Yet, even as the process of signing autographs has become an increasing burden and the intent of those seeking it less innocent, Nicklaus is a proactive and patient participant. It's common for Nicklaus to budget 30 minutes or more after a round to sign all the various mementos shoved in his face. "I have signed just about everything you can imagine," he said. And more than likely some things you can't.

Nicklaus learned by example early in his career the value of making time for supporters when he watched comedian Bob Hope dutifully honor request after request for pictures and autographs following a golf exhibition in Cincinnati.

"He saw how Bob handled people and it really made an impression on him," Barbara said.

During the four-hour flight from North Palm Beach to Scottsdale, Arizona, prior to the Tradition, Nicklaus burned half the time signing items that had been sent to him at Golden Bear International headquarters, signing probably more than 500 items. Fellow golfers are among the biggest collectors. The Bear tried to pay off a bet with Keith Fergus and Chris Perry after a Monday practice round at Muirfield. Nicklaus, who teamed with amateur Graeme Storm, had shot a solid 3-under-par 69 but lost the Nassau wager. After entering the grillroom, Nicklaus pulled out his money clip, the one he had won in a long drive contest in 1963 (with a clout of more than 341 yards—using a persimmon driver, no less), but the two men refused to accept anything more than a $20, signed, of course. Nicklaus inked the familiar script on them, the one with the ostentatious 'J' and huge, flowing 'N.' He also dated the bills. Perry held up his note to admire it. Fergus, a former Memorial champion, quickly buried his in his pocket.

"That's going in my trophy case," Fergus said, beaming.

After his great escape in Round 1, Nicklaus cut short his autograph session after 10 minutes, and couldn't stop apologizing to the assembled crowd. "I am so sorry guys, but I have to go," he said. "I will catch up with all of you tomorrow. I'm really sorry."

Not many great athletes would do that.

Nicklaus had a good reason for a hasty retreat to the clubhouse. He learned in the scorer's tent after completing play that Barbara, who had watched Gary shoot 72 in the morning wave, had become ill on the 14th hole. In fact, she was doubled over from the pain in her abdomen. Jackie asked her if she wanted him to go get help. When she said yes, he knew she must be ill; Barbara is obstinate when it comes to seeing doctors. Jackie, who had broken his heel seven months earlier in a boating accident, walked calmly down the cart path—until he rounded the corner out of sight. Then he sprinted to a first-aid station and eventually tracked down longtime family friend and physician, Jim Ryan. "It was the first time I'd run since I broke my foot," Jackie said. "I never ran so fast in my life."

Later that evening Barbara agreed to be taken to Ohio State University Medical Center. The diagnosis: kidney stones. The following day she underwent lithotripsy, a procedure that disintegrates the stones. She missed her first Memorial round, breaking an impressive streak in a family that knows their streaks. She missed a good day for the host family. Gary shot 68, ended a string of four weekends off, and trailed leader Tiger Woods, the defending champion, by six shots. Jack, after assurances from Barbara that he need not withdraw, bogeyed 17 and 18 for 73, but his 148 made the cut on the number. He was barely moved to smile by his performance, however. He was struggling to find his own wide fairways and his putting had become, in a word, inconvenient. He was fast running out of ways to fix it.

After the Compaq Classic, Nicklaus had revived a tried and true preparation tool in an effort to improve his scoring ability. He competed against himself. He would play nine holes at a time using two or three balls and keep score with each. Talk about the ultimate competition. Old Man Par didn't ever stand a chance.

But this time the practice didn't help. While watching playing partner Ernie Els shoot 64 amid docile conditions, Nicklaus managed his game meticulously and came up empty. He missed 10 makeable putts, including eight-footers at the last two holes. "I can't putt, I can't putt, I can't putt," he lamented time after time in the locker room. It summed up his day like he was writing it on a chalkboard as a way of self-punishment.

⌒

The Memorial Tournament traditionally is plagued by dark sky questions. The place is a magnet for thunderheads and other meteorological phenomenon, not to mention one-liners. The founder and host even said, "the only thing that would make this tournament better would be to put a dome over it."

Cold, sleet, lightning, rain, high winds, frost, snow…the Memorial has been staged in every condition imaginable. "We wanted weather to be a factor, sort of like at Augusta, but obviously we've gotten into a pattern that has been a little more (of a factor) than we could have imagined," Nicklaus said with frustration. Sixteen of the first 24 tournaments had at least one weather-related disruption and 22 of 96 rounds have been delayed, suspended, or canceled. Two of arguably the most impressive rounds of golf recorded in the last 25 years came amid horrid conditions at Muirfield. In the second round in 1979, Tom Watson shot 69 in winds gusting to 30 miles per hour and the wind-chill plummeting to 13 degrees. Forty-two players failed to break 80 and the field scoring average was 78.738. Fred Couples cobbled together an opening 69 in similar weather in 1990. His was four shots better than the next best score as the field set a record with a 78.792 scoring average.

Saturday's tee times were moved forward and threesomes were sent off both tees to beat an approaching storm front that once more was headed for Dublin. The rain held off while the unflappable Barbara Nicklaus returned to the galleries and saw portions of Jack's 72, his first round of par or better at Muirfield in three years, and Gary's 74. Under lift, clean, and place rules, Woods shot a 65 to retain his six-stroke margin, the largest 54-hole lead in tournament history.

Jack spent the better part of two hours on the range after Saturday's round as the weather continued to hold off. While his putting was a source of unabated frustration, he spent the majority of time beating drivers in preparation for the narrow U.S. Open strips he would encounter at Pebble Beach. Nicklaus fiddled with different clubs, lead tape on the clubs, and incremental swing adjustments in an attempt to find that consistent fade he knew he must have to be competitive. There was just no rediscovering that reliable shot pattern, and its elusiveness left him agitated as he packed up for the day.

The forecast for Sunday called for light rain, so naturally, play was washed out after a two-inch deluge, forcing the tournament's third

Monday finish and second in four years. Nicklaus, who in the wet, soft conditions wasn't being tested as much as he'd have hoped, was 1 over par through 11 holes when play was halted and that's what he ended up with Monday morning, a 1-over 73 and a 5-over 293 total, tied for 63rd place. Gary, meanwhile, came back with a 71-285 to finish 25th.

Woods won going away with a closing 70 and 269 total, one off Tom Lehman's tournament record. He became the first repeat Memorial winner and joined a distinguished list of multiple winners that include Nicklaus, Watson, Greg Norman, and Hale Irwin.

Nicklaus traditionally sits in on the champion's interview and it turned into an occasion for the first serious comparisons between the two men while they were in each other's presence. Nicklaus, probably the best interview in the game, if not in all of sports, was unfailingly gracious and as always offered relevant observations, even as worries of his own game were percolating underneath the surface. His face was drawn. He looked exhausted. It had been a long week of physical and mental stress.

Nicklaus credited Woods for improving his distance control, for his ability to hit his tee shots long and shape them the way he wants to into certain areas of the fairway. He said Woods' short game "is phenomenal, and he is a terrific putter."

A questioner asked about Woods' game in comparison to Nicklaus' of 20 years ago.

"Thirty years ago, maybe," Nicklaus replied to laughter. "I see a lot of similarities. I always felt like everybody else was going to play for second. And I think he feels the same way. When he's doing what he wants to do, he knows and believes in his own mind, as I did, that ... we were going to win."

Another questioner asked Woods, does any other place set up as well for your game (as Muirfield)?

"Probably Augusta," Woods said.

"Pebble?" Jack interjected, prompting more laughter.

"Pebble," Woods agreed. "True, I've had some pretty low rounds at Pebble. A 63 and two 64s there."

Nicklaus closed his eyes and shook his head. Woods would be the overwhelming favorite at the U.S. Open and set his sights on yet another Nicklaus feat, the Pebble Beach double.

Nicklaus, meanwhile, was still trying to find his feet. His putting he classified as "mediocre," and his driving "atrocious, the worst I've ever driven the ball." Being that these were the two key components to his marvelous success, his somber mood was understandable. He was not achieving the kind of progress he had hoped for.

"I've worked pretty hard this spring to try to get my golf game somewhat respectable and I was respectable for a couple of rounds at Augusta and fell on my face, you might say, the last two rounds. I'd like to not have that happen at the Open.

"I've worked at it pretty hard. But I've worked at the darned game for 40 years…and, frankly, I'm tired of that. Your body can't take it."

Nicklaus wasn't saying he was tired of golf, nor did his actions suggest that. But discovering solutions for his golf had never before proved so elusive, and he was wearying of that circumstance. It was gnawing at him in a way you would expect after years of having his game respond to his requests.

Of course, before he left Ohio, he vowed to work just a little harder still. He continues to live by the lessons learned from his father: never give up; never stop striving for excellence—no matter the obstacles. Soon he would depart for the West Coast, and one could only wonder if his entry onto 17 Mile Drive heading to Pebble Beach would help him turn back the odometer once again—in the same way as when he eagerly drove up Magnolia Lane.

"I'm doing more things well than I've done for a few years, but it's a funny game, it really is," he said with a trace of wonder. Yes, after all these years the game still fascinates him. "You lose confidence with something and you turn right around and have to face it and that's just sort of the fate of things. The game has a certain fate to it that you accept. You cut your wrists and put them together and say, 'What time tomorrow?'"

6

WAVES

SEA CHANGE AT PEBBLE BEACH

As a prelude to the centennial U.S. Open at Pebble Beach Golf Links, the June 11 edition of the *Monterey County Herald* splashed a perfunctory feature story over most of the front of Section C, its lead sports page. It was the kind of typical article that newspapers produce for special occasions, done primarily for posterity. This story was entitled: "Cornerstones of the kingdom: 10 who shaped golf on the Monterey Peninsula." Its list appeared alphabetically rather than in order of importance and impact, which was sort of like laying up on a par-4. Such a list would have been so easy and fun to do, not to mention instructive.

It evoked a rudimentary question: Who were the *most* important figures?

You start with Samuel F.B. Morse. In 1915, Morse had the foresight to build a golf course along a pristine stretch of coastline off Carmel Bay instead of developing a subdivision of 50-by-100 foot lots, as first considered. Without Morse there would be no kingdom in the Del Monte Forest. Jack Neville, the California Amateur champion who, with an assist from fellow amateur Douglas Grant, carved the coast into magnificent Pebble Beach Golf Links. He was the initial architect of that kingdom. Bing Crosby was its first ambassador, throwing a spotlight on the Monterey Peninsula in 1947 when he moved the national Pro-Am tournament from Rancho Santa Fe Country Club in San Diego to Pebble Beach, Cypress Point, and Monterey Peninsula Country Club.

Logically, Jack Nicklaus made the list, and after Morse, Neville, and Crosby, you could argue that no one had a bigger impact on golf on the Monterey Peninsula than the Golden Bear. He owns the key to the kingdom; he wears the crown.

If he had one round of golf to play, Nicklaus said it would not be at Augusta National or his own Muirfield Village. Nor would he cross the Atlantic Ocean to St. Andrews. He would choose Pebble Beach. He has been enamored with the course since he first saw it prior to the 1961 U.S. Amateur. Of all the many honors bestowed upon him, being selected to design the new par-3 fifth hole along Stillwater Cove ranks among the highest. Constructed on a little more than half of a previously unavailable 5.5 acres, the new hole, playing 188 yards and most receptive to a gentle fade (if you can imagine that), made its debut to rave reviews in 1998 and added one more of his large paw prints to the beloved landscape in Northern California.

"There are probably better golf courses than Pebble Beach," explained Nicklaus, who has also overseen numerous other renovations on the golf course. "But because of where it sits and what it's been in my life, I really don't care whether there are better golf courses."

Riviera Country Club was dubbed Hogan's Alley after Ben Hogan won consecutive L.A. Opens there in 1947-48 and returned to capture the '48 U.S. Open. Nicklaus pulled his own Hogan in 1972-73 with a wire-to-wire win in the '72 Open at Pebble Beach sandwiched between back-to-back victories in the Bing Crosby National Pro-Am. In that first Open staged at Pebble, Nicklaus matched Bobby Jones' record with his 13th major championship, won the second leg of the grand slam, and orchestrated one of the most memorable shots in championship history—a heat-seeking 1-iron that hit the flagstick at the par-3 17th to set up a tap-in birdie on the 71st hole.

So it's no stretch to say Pebble Beach might be thought of as Nicklaus Harbor.

Augmenting his Pebble parcel is the '61 U.S. Amateur, the tournament where he first walked off yardages (a practice that soon after became standard on the PGA Tour), three Crosby Clambakes in all, and two wins in Shell's Wonderful World of Golf (over Sam Snead and Tom Watson more than 30 years apart).

Pebble Beach. Nicklaus Harbor.

"I've developed quite a love affair with Pebble Beach," he said. "It's as dramatic as any course in the country, but mostly it was the complete test of golf that intrigued me."

There could not be a more appropriate place for Nicklaus to end his incredible string of 44 straight U.S. Open starts—if indeed it was going to end. For if Pebble Beach represented a complete test of golf, the national open championship always represented to Nicklaus the most important, because he is an American, and the most defining, because of its difficulty. In a way, the U.S. Open was made for Nicklaus and players of his ilk like Hogan, another four-time champion. No tournament places a greater emphasis on par, and perhaps no player understood the value of par better than Nicklaus.

"The U.S. Open, to me, is a total examination of the game of golf, the way the course is set up, what is done and I think...to a golfer it probably does more to make a man out of you than any other tournament."

Nicklaus relished this crucible. "I enjoy the punishment. I suppose I must be a masochist of some kind but I enjoy that."

Over a span of six decades Nicklaus established himself as the man among men in golf's toughest test. He competed in his first Open as a precocious 17-year-old, nearly won it as a 20-year-old amateur in 1960, and made the championship his first professional title in 1962. He would go on to win four, finish runner-up four more times, and post 11 top-five and 18 top-10 finishes, though the last of those was in 1986. Twenty-two times he placed among the top 25.

He enjoyed three separate stretches of phenomenal consistency and eerie omnipresence from which he extracted three wins. From 1966-68, Nicklaus was out of the top 10 only twice after the 12 completed rounds, and he won in '67 at Baltusrol. He bested Palmer with a decisive 65 and record 275 total and eclipsed the previous mark held by Hogan. From 1980-82 he was out of the top 10 once and won again at Baltusol in '80—again setting the 72-hole record with a 272 total and becoming the second man to win the Open twice on the same course. (Willie Anderson at Myopia Hunt Club in 1901 and '05 is the other.) Then there was 1971-73, the most fruitful period of Nicklaus' career. In 12 U.S. Open rounds, he remained among the top 10 after each round, and only once, when he stood ninth after the third round in '73, did he stray from the top five.

Not to be overlooked is the fact that the latter two periods included trips to Pebble Beach. In the total examination of the U.S. Open, on the most complete test of a layout, Nicklaus exuded supreme confidence and displayed unvarnished brilliance.

⌐

The USGA held one other Open at Pebble Beach prior to 2000, in 1992, which was won by Tom Kite. Nicklaus, after turning 50 years old, missed only three Open cuts in the decade—and you can throw out 1999, when he played at about 60 percent strength after his hip surgery and appeared in just one major. In '92 he struggled to 77-74-151.

The struggle might have been as much—or more—internal as anything else.

In 1991, as the number of rounds of golf proliferated on the famed layout—even as greens fees spiraled upward to their present level of $300 (for guests at the Lodge)—officials of the Pebble Beach Co. decided to convert Pebble's turf from its native fescues and Kikuyu to perennial rye. Rye grass regenerates in a week. Because American golfers, brainwashed as much as anything by Augusta National's agronomic practices, define perfect conditions in the narrowest of parameters (lush and green), that's what they expect to see on a golf course for which they're shelling out multiple C-notes.

Rye grass, however, is as native to the seascape as an icicle at the equator. Combined with the stringent USGA setup of narrow fairways, marble greens, and rough measuring three inches or more, this made for an artificiality that Nicklaus accepted strictly on a practical level.

"What's happened to Pebble Beach is not something I'm real happy with. I'm not sure the USGA is either, but I'm not sure what the alternative is," he said prior to the championship. "I think the rye grass has improved the fairways, but…I'm going to contradict myself a little…there is no natural rye grass on the Monterey Peninsula and I do not like that the rye grass has turned it into inland conditions. I understand the problem when you're playing some thousands of rounds, but this is a seaside golf course and should play like one."

As he summed up his feelings on the subject, he began to smile. "They changed the golf course I won on. Shame on them," he mocked.

In the end it didn't matter. It was still Pebble, which along with St. Andrews he calls, "those two guiding lights." And it was still the U.S. Open, the brightest beacon through all his sensational summers.

He'd find out soon enough just where the lights were guiding him. As always, he knew where he wanted to go. It had been a road traveled many times before, and many times he had reached his destination.

"My expectations are always too high," he said, estimating his chances at 1000-1. "I never thought that age made any difference, but I'm starting to think differently. Just starting. But I'm foolish enough to think I can win the golf tournament, yet I know I'm not playing well. I always believe that somewhere inside me I have a chance to do that."

⌒

Nicklaus arrived early for his 44th Open, flying to Monterey on Friday evening June 9. He enjoyed a leisurely practice round Saturday afternoon with Jackie, Jim Lipe, and Scott Tolley. Well, it was leisurely for everyone but Tolley. His wife, Tamara, had just given birth to their first son, Dylan, four days earlier, and it was difficult for him to assess whether labor pains or five-plus nervous hours on a golf course with his boss was easier to endure.

Tolley, athletic, with weightlifter's shoulders, is a decent player. Possessing good power off the tee, he carries close to a single digit handicap, impressive considering how little he plays. But playing with the Golden Bear was an intimidating proposition without the added burden of trying on little sleep to negotiate a devious golf course, one that in a week's time would prevent all but one of the 156 Open competitors from breaking par. The occasional interruption by the likes of Arnold Palmer, who recently had become an owner of Pebble Beach and its related properties (including Spyglass Hill and Spanish Bay), and NBC golf announcers Roger Maltbie and Johnny Miller only compounded the pressure.

Needless to say, Tolley was reduced to apologizing his way around the 6,846-yard layout. It was perfectly understandable. Nicklaus understood. After watching his director of communications flail away for nine holes, he finally stepped in to calm him. Tolley teed up his ball on the difficult 10th, which skirts the cliffs above the Pacific Ocean, but Nicklaus picked it up and re-teed it for him. He then looked Tolley in the eyes and said, "This is your hole."

For a few moments there was a transfer of power. Tolley unleashed a terrific drive, made par, and won the hole.

"It was the weirdest thing," Tolley would later relay. "He touches the golf ball and it's like he has put a magic spell on it or something."

Magic is as good an explanation as any for what Nicklaus accomplished over the years with an inferior brand of golf ball. Contractually obligated to MacGregor, Nicklaus used its Tourney golf ball for the majority of his career. Officials at the USGA, which administers the Rules of Golf in the United States, Canada, and Mexico and also regulates equipment, had not long before the 100th Open tested that ball. They were amazed by what they discovered. Frank Thomas, recently retired as USGA technical director, apprised Nicklaus of the results.

"The USGA told me, 'We tested all those golf balls, and they were 20 yards shorter (than others); and one went 20 yards right and one 20 yards left. How you could win tournaments with that golf ball, (we) won't ever know. It's the worst ball ever made.'"

One can only wonder what Nicklaus might have accomplished with a golf ball of modern quality tailored aerodynamically to his game. How much more impressive might his major championship record be? After all, he lost nine championships by two shots or less, and a 10th, the 1971 U.S. Open at Merion, he lost in a playoff to Lee Trevino.

None of that is of any interest to Nicklaus, however. "Water over the dam," he said when the question arose. "I don't pay attention to that. I only worry about the water going over the dam right now. That's the only water I can control."

Nicklaus got in practice rounds Monday and Wednesday, but put the clubs aside Tuesday to rest a nagging stiff neck. He opted for a long walk with Barbara at nearby Spanish Bay. Later that evening the couple attended the first U.S. Open Past Champions Dinner at the Beach Club just off Pebble's fourth hole. Twenty former champions, from 88-year-old Byron Nelson to 30-year-old Ernie Els, joined the celebration, which was the brainchild of Jerry Pate, the '76 Open winner. Filet mignon and the retelling of their respective fairy tales were on the menu.

Beforehand, they posed together for a keepsake photograph that should go for an obscene amount on e-Bay if anyone can garner all 20 signatures. The camera captures Palmer and Nelson flanking the Open trophy. Behind them, hovering dead center over the top of it, is Nicklaus.

The Monday practice round pairing of Nicklaus and Tom Watson, the '82 Open protagonists, highlighted the pretournament proceedings. It was hard to fathom that 18 years had passed since Nicklaus, certain that a record fifth national title was his, watched in stunned incredulity as Watson chipped in for birdie at the 17th hole from what looked to be an almost impossible position.

Nicklaus had never had the opportunity, much less the inclination, to gather the details of the 16-foot sand wedge chip Watson executed, but as they approached the 17th green on this day, Nicklaus' curiosity got the best of him. He inquired about the exact spot from which Watson dealt him his most bitter setback. Watson headed to the upper left portion of the shallow, hourglass-shaped green and with his putter pointed to an area above where the flagstick was located that June afternoon in 1982. Watson reminded him that the lie was providentially perfect.

"Well," Nicklaus said, "that makes a little bit of a difference as far as the difficulty of the shot."

"He saw that it made it (look) a little easier," Watson said later with a broad smile, a bit of pride showing through even now. "The pain was not as tough to take after 18 years."

Much would be made later in the week, and in subsequent majors, of the figurative passing of the baton from Nicklaus to Tiger Woods as the game's dominant player. Nicklaus maintained that he had passed it long ago. Indeed he had, but it wasn't voluntarily. Watson, with that inspired chip shot, yanked it from his grasp.

⌒

Eighteen years ago Jack Nicklaus would not have been seen conducting a grand opening for one of his golf course designs the week of a major championship, but there he was on the Sunday prior at Pasadera Country Club, proudly showing off his first 18-hole design on the Monterey Peninsula.

He had reason to be proud.

Set in the hills above the Del Monte Forest, Pasadera offers a wondrous natural canvas. It possesses a number of dramatic elevation changes (up to 375 feet) and offers sweeping vistas of the peninsula as it weaves through a 565-acre residential development. The par-71 layout, the 190th to Nicklaus' credit at that time, measures 6,801 yards from the championship tees. That the routing was predetermined presented an unusual challenge. In most instances residential lots are plotted after a course routing has been established, but just the opposite occurred at Pasadera. Nevertheless, Nicklaus and Jim Lipe made the most of what they had.

Jackie joined his father for the ceremonial first round and even recorded the first birdie, at the fourth hole. It was the start of a huge week for the literal "next Nicklaus." Jack William Nicklaus II, who was days away from joining the American Society of Golf Course Architects, had intended to caddie for his father in all four majors in 2000. Steve, two years younger, caught wind of the deal just before the year began and lobbied for a split of duties.

Jackie, 39, chose the Masters and the U.S. Open, leaving Steve with the British Open and PGA. It was a civil, adult, amicable process—nothing like their years growing up. Their childhood battles were intense, one of them ending when Jackie, about 11 at the time, evaded Steve, butcher knife in hand, by stealing away at the end of the boat dock. But the boys have bonded sufficiently since. In fact, the entire Nicklaus clan that includes Nan, Gary, Michael, the spouses and 12 grandchildren remains exceedingly tight-knit.

"The kids are what I'm most proud of," said Nicklaus, who off the top of his head can rattle off the birthdays of each of his grandchildren. "We didn't know when Jackie and Steve were growing up if one of them was going to live past 20. Now they live two doors down from each other and are plotting on how they can get the house in between and knock it down and live closer. All five kids are within a few miles of Barbara and me, and that is what's great."

Born just after the 1961 Amateur, Jackie's life practically spans his father's professional career. His memories, among the five Nicklaus children, are the most vivid and comprehensive, his life most directly impacted by his dad's unparalleled success. The pressures of being Jack Nicklaus Jr. must have been enormous growing up (they probably have only abated slightly as he follows in his dad's footsteps as an architect), yet he never shrank from the implicit burden. Even as a tyke he seemed to grasp his special identity. Asked what his name was, the Bear cub would respond, "Jackie Nicklaus Under Par." Polite, charming, and reflexively witty—not to mention a merciless prankster, which Jack insists was instilled in him by Barbara—Jack II has emerged as a respected ambassador of the game and his family.

Jackie shot a respectable 74 at Pasadera, two more than the architect, but he wasn't paying that much attention to his game. He was continually checking his dad's swing. On the 10th hole, a par 5, Jackie launched a huge drive. His father busted it a few yards farther. They remained on the tee discussing shoulder rotation.

"That was the best part of my game," Nicklaus said to his son. "I could get my left shoulder back and load up and I could stay back there for a half hour. Now I can't be there one-eighth of a second. I don't have the patience. Your game changes. You change."

One thing that never changes is a rally by the Bear over the closing holes, the ability to give a proper sendoff. He birdied 17 and 18 and his final stroke was a 40-footer from the fringe that he predicted would go in. Nicklaus made sure to sign the scorecard for posterity. It was to be put on display in the clubhouse along with the persimmon driver with which he teed off on the first hole. "Nice keepsakes; wish I could take them home," someone was overhead saying.

∽

The most famous scorecard of Nicklaus' career at Pebble Beach is not the one from the '72 Open. It is one that dates to before the 1961 Amateur. At the suggestion of Deane Beman, Nicklaus walked off yardages on the golf course prior to the championship, making his notations on a scorecard. Nicklaus still possesses that scorecard, which he said was useful for about 15 years, until most of the landmarks disappeared. He modified it slightly for the '72 Open, probably the last time it had relevancy. But Nicklaus doesn't need the scorecard to tell you what's on it. His elephant-like memory is enough. Give him five minutes and he can rattle off the Pebble Beach of yesteryear, the one without yardages on sprinkler heads. In his own words, here is how he once broke down Nicklaus Harbor:

"On the first hole I played off the left bunker, usually with an iron, and from there I had it 138 (yards) to the front of the green and 162 to the back.

"The second hole, the bunker on the right was 199 yards to the front and 222 to the back of the green off of that.

"On the third hole, the sprinkler in the middle of the fairway opposite the big tree on the left was 135 to the front, 160 to the back.

"At four I had to change the marker pretty soon after (the Amateur). I used to use the start of the bunker on the left, which was 102 yards to the front.

"Five and seven, they are whatever they are, depending on hole location and tee markers.

"At eight I used the edge of the cliff. I walked to the edge of the cliff for the distance. After a while I thought that was probably not smart. From the center of the fairway off the edge of the cliff was like 147 to the green.

"At nine I always used two trees in Crosby's old yard near his bay window. There were once two trees near Crosby's old house right of 13 and when you got to those in the middle of the fairway at the ninth it was 187 to the front and 213 to the back.

"At the 10th, you hit it to the first bunker on the right and it was 156 to the front and 180 to the back. This is gone now but there was an opening to the bushes on the right at 11 and it was 122 yards to the front of the green and 144 to the back.

"At 12, from the front of the back, it has always been 185 yards.

"Used the same trees at 13 as I did on nine and the yardages were 113 and 138. I miss those trees," he sighed.

"At 14, you probably don't remember, but there was a tree struck by lightning to the right of the fairway. Arnold hit the tree and the ball went out-of-bounds. (It was in the '67 Crosby, won by Nicklaus, and Palmer in pursuit, hit the tree twice and lost two balls.) That night the tree was struck by lightning and fell down. From that particular tree it was 99 yards to the front of the green.

"There's a second oak tree on the right at 15, I can still use that. That's 156 and 180.

"From the start of the first bunker on the right at 16, it was 134 yards to the front and 160 to the back.

"At 18 I used to try to get home in two. Haven't for a while. There was a tree that's gone now on the left side of the fairway. If you drove it out past that tree there was a sprinkler right beside it and that was 232 to the front. That was my go range."

Nicklaus apologized that his figures might be off a yard or two, which is unlikely. "Not that it matters," he then added with a tinge of regret. "The reference points just aren't there."

And if they were?

"I can't play Pebble Beach the way I used to play it anyway," he shrugged. "I've played Pebble pretty much the same way all my life. There are just certain things I don't do on that golf course anymore. Mainly, I can't reach any of the par-5 holes in two shots anymore. But there's a lot of lay up at Pebble Beach. I guess I'll play Pebble the same way I always have."

⌒

The U.S. Open tradition of pairing the defending champion with the reigning U.S. Amateur champion and British Open champion was established in 1980, the year of Nicklaus' fourth and final Open triumph. For the second time in his career Nicklaus found himself as a member of that notable trio.

This occasion was different, however. In fact, it was unlike any other in the 100-year history of the championship. Nicklaus was taking the place of the late Payne Stewart, who perished the week before the Tour Championship, four months after winning the 99th U.S. Open at Pinehurst No. 2 in North Carolina. In one of the more memorable and emotionally charged major championship finishes, Stewart, at age 42, had won his second Open title by one stroke over Phil Mickelson with a 15-foot par putt on the 72nd hole. It allowed him to atone for his runner-up finish to Lee Janzen in '98 at Olympic Club in San Francisco, when he had led after each of the first three rounds. Stewart became only the fifth man to triumph one year after coming in second. The last man to do it was Nicklaus—in 1972—at Pebble Beach after losing in a play-off to Trevino at Merion.

There could have been no more appropriate choice for the honor of spelling Stewart than the four-time champion. Following his victory at Pinehurst, Stewart had reflected on his winning 15-foot par putt on the 72nd green. It brought back memories of his childhood golfing days, of his imaginary conquests. "I liked to think I was Jack Nicklaus," Stewart had said. "The same thing on the putting green. 'I'm going to be Jack today. I'm going to make this one and win the U.S. Open.'"

On this cool afternoon Jack Nicklaus now was standing in for Payne Stewart.

⌒

Stewart's death, not to mention subsequent related developments, had a profound impact on Nicklaus. With his effacing wit, Stewart was somewhat of a kindred spirit, someone Nicklaus appreciated on several levels. But that plane crash hit home further for Nicklaus when he learned soon after that one of the other four passengers on that charter flight was Bruce Borland, a senior associate with Nicklaus Design. Among his ongoing projects were The King & The Bear site. Borland was accompanying Stewart to Dallas, where the two men were to collaborate on Stewart's first design project. Stewart, who had matriculated from Southern Methodist University, was then to fly on to Houston.

Nicklaus spends nearly as much time in his airplane as he does at home, so the Stewart accident naturally spooked him, although he never had encountered a serious problem in his own planes. In 1993, en route via helicopter from Columbus to Dayton for a site visit at Country Club of the North, the aircraft was forced down by fog. It landed without incident in a cornfield north of Springfield, next to a golf course.

Just a few weeks after the Stewart accident, however, Nicklaus absorbed another jolt when Roy Ricks, the president of his apparel company, perished in a private plane crash outside of Chicago. "That one got to him a bit," Ron Hurst said. "He would not be human if it hadn't, especially for as much as he flies. It makes you think."

After several days of record heat on the Monterey Peninsula, the weather for the opening round on Thursday, June 15, reverted to its more normal cool and overcast conditions—and, spookily, not unlike the gauzy mist that enveloped the final round at Pinehurst.

Nicklaus was due to tee off at 12:40 p.m. with amateur champ David Gossett and Don Pooley. The first alternate, Pooley had replaced British Open winner Paul Lawrie, who withdrew due to a groin injury. However, around noon, tee times were delayed by the USGA because a six-group backup had developed at the par-3 fifth, Nicklaus' hole. With Stillwater Cove perilously close on the right, Nicklaus designed the replacement par 3 with a bailout chipping area left of the putting surface. But the USGA tournament committee decided to take that area away by growing it to the same height of the rough. This relegated the players to a chop or hack from the deep stuff to a green running toward the water, a nearly impossible shot. Ranked the sixth most difficult hole of the week at 3.381 strokes, the fifth was a speed bump that yielded just 27 birdies compared to 138 bogeys.

Having to wait nearly an hour from the completion of his warm-up to his first tee shot did nothing for Nicklaus' creaky back and neck, or for his emotions, which he had been fighting to keep in check. He lost the battle when it finally was his turn to play. Teeing off third, he had decided to dedicate a moment of silence to Stewart, who also had been honored the previous morning with golf's version of a 21-gun salute. Two waves of golfers—more than 40 players—launched tee shots in synchronization into the Pacific during a brief sunrise ceremony Wednesday on the 18th fairway.

Nicklaus stood behind his ball with his head bowed. Then he lined up his shot only to false start and return to his golf bag. He wiped his eyes with a towel and then tried to refocus.

"What was that?" Tolley asked in a whisper of concern.

It was Nicklaus, for maybe the first time in his career, standing on the first tee of a major championship and struggling to get his mind solely on the championship. It was Nicklaus letting more of his true self emerge from behind that oft-seen countenance of concentration—the man whom his mother said "always has been emotional, but he just doesn't let you see it."

You could see it now.

"I was taking Payne's place as it relates to that starting time ... so I told (starter) Ron Read I was going to give him a moment of silence. I didn't expect that much emotion to come after that. Then I couldn't get my mind on the shot."

His 3-wood darted left into the rough. He had to lay up short and he couldn't convert from 14 feet to save his par. The second hole, converted from a par-5 to a par-4 for the championship, was almost a carbon copy: pulled drive, lay up, pitch, two putts from eight feet. But he holed a 20-footer for par at the third and settled down to go out in 37. He was gaining momentum. But he would go no farther.

The clash of cool ocean air with the traces of the retreating warm front produced a soupy fog that rolled in quickly and blanketed the golf course. Visibility diminished rapidly to less than 100 yards on most holes. Play was suspended at 3:56 p.m. Pacific time with 75 golfers still on the course. Nicklaus was perplexed by the turn of events. He wanted to continue. "I haven't been able to see that far for years, so it doesn't bother me."

⤳

Nicklaus arose at 4:15 a.m. Friday to prepare to complete his opening round, not a happy hour for a man who likes his sleep. By the time he arrived at the practice range to prepare for the 6:30 restart it was packed with golfers. Many were forced to wait for a spot to become available, but everyone inched closer together to make room for the Golden Bear.

As it should be for the monarch in his kingdom.

After fog further delayed a restart to 7:45, Nicklaus managed to pick up where he left off, steering his way around the familiar grounds without much trouble, but also void of much spark. He played the back nine in even par with one birdie, at the 11th after a 9-iron to 2 feet, and one bogey for a two-over 73. Asked if he was satisfied, Nicklaus, in typical Bear fashion, replied, "I'm never satisfied to be eight shots back."

As always, Nicklaus relates everything to his competitive standing, and he didn't think much of where he stood when Tiger Woods, who was among the more fortunate with an early-late tee schedule, had been able to fashion a fairly effortless, bogey-free 65, the lowest Open round ever produced at Pebble Beach.

Nicklaus had work to do and the task came calling quickly. He, Gossett, and Pooley had 35 minutes between the completion of their first round and the start of the second. As the oldest man in the field, Nicklaus, though he refused to believe it, stood to be the most adversely affected by 27 humbling holes of golf. It didn't take long for indicators of distress to appear.

He was forced to lay up again at the converted 484-yard, par-4 second hole and made another bogey, but the real trouble began when he pulled his tee shot left at the par-3 fifth. The ball caromed off a spectator's back and kicked farther left. Nicklaus needed two chips to reach the green and two putts to get down.

Suddenly, he was five over par. To make matters worse, the skies cleared, bringing sunshine and freshening breezes. Pebble was becoming ever more enigmatical. "That was the first time I thought about not making the cut," he said. The long walk to the sixth tee got just a bit longer.

There was more heartache at the eighth. Nicklaus loves the eighth hole. It is among his favorites in golf, and the second shot over the cliff is his favorite. "I get excited just getting it in the fairway there to set up that shot," he said. Following the flight of his 3-wood tee shot to its apex, Nicklaus was feeling excited again. It was a solid hit, striped right down the middle. But he was aghast when he found it teetering on the ledge of the chasm. He could do nothing but take a drop with a penalty, though he briefly inched toward the ledge to test a stance while Jackie hung onto his belt, a move that had the crowd yelling nervously for him to abandon the move. His next stroke was as good as the last, a pure 7-iron that was all over the flagstick. But the ball flew over the green into deep rough. His downhill chip had no chance of settling close after it hit the fringe collar and darted forward down the slope, 40 feet away.

"That epitomized his round," Jackie said flatly.

"I hit three good shots and made a double-bogey," Jack added. "I knew then it wasn't my day."

The message had been delivered as subtly as a hammer to the thumb. On the fifth hole, the one he built, and the eighth, perhaps his favorite par-4, he could not have been more rudely received by the golf gods.

"At that point," he added, "I figured I had better enjoy the last nine holes for a reason other than playing tomorrow."

Outside the ropes, Barbara was carrying a Beanie Baby bear someone in the gallery had given her, but it brought no luck. She fingered a roll of pennies and flipped them in various heads-tails combinations. Nothing worked. Jack missed the ninth green, made bogey and turned in 6-over-par 41.

The back nine may have been as bittersweet as any Nicklaus had ever traversed. The word had gotten out that the Bear was in the midst of his last lap and the size of the gallery appeared to have tripled by the time he reached 11 and turned toward home. "Let's go watch Jack up these last few holes to 18. Let's go watch some history," said one spectator, echoing thoughts shared by thousands. But the people didn't just watch. The admiration they poured forth was overwhelming. They stood on every hole. It only made Nicklaus want to try harder than ever. But as he dug down he only found himself in a deeper hole.

As the winds increased in intensity, the fairways turned to ribbons. The greens became mirages. Pebble Beach was at its evil best. Nicklaus missed eight more greens in succession (and 23 in 36 holes) and bogeyed five holes. He wasn't playing poorly, but he was off just enough to suffer poor results. It didn't matter. The cheers grew increasingly ardent. "I enjoyed it," Nicklaus admitted later. "I would have liked to have played a little bit better, but I enjoyed the last few holes in spite of what I was shooting."

⌐

Upon reaching the 18th tee, which juts into Carmel Bay, Nicklaus wandered to the far left side of the tee near the cliff, got a drink of water, then hoisted his left leg on the split-rail fence that guards the edge. He sat quietly for a minute, gazing into the Pacific. "I wanted to take a last look," he explained. His eyes fixed on something far, far away, but the emotions were beginning to roll in and crash over him as he pondered the finish.

> ... *"We have lingered in the chambers of the sea,*
> *By sea-girls wreathed with seaweed red and brown*
> *Till human voices wake us, and we drown."*

—T.S. Eliot

It was at that crystallizing moment he decided to exit the Open with a bang and not a whimper.

"You know," Jack said to Jackie upon returning to his white golf bag, "I haven't tried to knock it on the green in two shots here in over 20 years. Let's see if we can knock it on in two today."

He gripped his 9-degree driver, the one made by his own equipment company, and ripped a drive left of the aging, slumping Cypress tree in the middle of the 18th fairway. There used to be two of them huddled together against the unceasing breeze, but one was lost in 1999 to pitch canker and the remaining tree was expected to succumb to the same fate soon.

The majestic 18th hole at Pebble Beach is 545 yards. Nicklaus' clout left him 238 yards to the front edge of the green and 261 yards to the hole. It was just outside the "go range" marked on the scorecard of his youth. But now his defiance kicked in against the antagonism of age.

After Pooley and Gossett hit short of the green, Nicklaus took a mighty lash with his metal 3-wood. The ball sailed high and drew smartly toward the narrow opening of the green, holding its line into a stiff, quartering crosswind. The ball bounced twice before rolling onto the putting surface.

The world exploded.

The sequence of shots called to mind the last at-bat of Boston Red Sox slugger Ted Williams. In 1960, the Splendid Splinter, in his final plate appearance, at his beloved Fenway Park, jacked a home run.

This is how the great ones, the lords of sport, take their bows.

On the practice putting green, leader Tiger Woods, who was about to begin his second round, heard the mammoth roar. He turned to Butch Harmon, his swing coach, and smiled. "Jack is due to finish any time now," he pointed out.

Woods, scheduled to go off at 4:40 p.m., asked a photographer nearby what had happened. He called an associate on his radio. "Who is it?"

The reply: "It's Jack."

"If this was his last U.S. Open it would have been nice to have actually seen it," Woods, who already had the tournament by the throat, explained later. "But I had more important things to take care of."

Indeed, just as Jack Nicklaus was closing his Open career, Tiger Woods was beginning his journey into championship lore, and was on his way to copying Nicklaus' Pebble Beach double. He would go on to set or tie a slew of records with his 12-under-par 272 effort, including the largest winning margin—15 strokes—in major championship history.

Such correlation in time and space between the two men, their two destinies, was too eerily synchronized to be mere coincidence.

As Nicklaus began the long final walk up the 18th fairway—his 2,930th U.S. Open hole covering 160 rounds—the championship all but came to a standstill. NBC, which televises the USGA championships, diverted most of its handheld cameras to the Golden Bear and the seascape. "It was always our intent that when Jack was playing 18 everything else was going to come to a halt for us," NBC golf producer Tommy Roy said.

With his cap off and his guard down, Nicklaus moved in his usual swift gait toward the green.

The human voices awoke.

Then came the drowning—of cheers and of tears.

About 5,000 fans in the grandstand right of the green rose to their feet and offered wave upon wave of applause so thunderous and moving that the tide seemed to roll out of Carmel Bay. There was a multitude of shouts. "One more year!" and "We love you, Jack." And this: "Say it ain't so, Jack!"

Barbara was thinking the same thing. Say it ain't so. "I didn't let myself think about it," she said after it was over, dabbing at corners of her eyes, the ones with the broken spigots. "I was preparing myself for a real emotional day, but on Sunday. *That* was supposed to be the last day."

Nicklaus, weary, achy, and sad, waved his left hand to the worshiping throngs surrounding the green, and upon reaching his ball, he pointed down at it and then pointed at his chest, as if to ask, "Can this be mine?" The gallery broke up.

Back in the fairway, Tom Watson joined in the applause then accepted a towel from his caddie, Bruce Edwards, and wiped his eyes. "You just have to give the man his due," said Watson, who after completing play exchanged hugs with the Bear. "The crowd was giving him a standing 'O' and I had to give him a standing 'O' too, because I have such great respect for what he has done for the game."

Isao Aoki, vanquished by Nicklaus in 1980 in a riveting Open at Baltusrol, also wept. Working as a commentator for Japan's TV Asahi, Aoki's voice simply failed him. Pooley lost his composure. "To be a part of that scene and to know what he has meant to golf, you'd have to be a rock not to have it affect you," he said.

Nicklaus, no rock, was rapidly faltering, too. As he dutifully studied his eagle putt of some 50 feet, the moisture in his eyes refused to subside and his contacts were almost useless. "He said they were floating," Jackie said.

He topped the putt, leaving it 10 feet short. He turned his brown and blue cap sideways like a baseball clown. He and Jackie then shared a laugh when his son insisted he read his own last putt. Jack saw right edge. Jackie concurred. Still glassy-eyed, the Bear nudged the putt up the hill, but it stopped on the lip. "Where are the golf gods when you need them?" NBC anchor Dan Hicks asked from the broadcast booth. Nicklaus spun away from the defiant ball in disgust before tapping in. It was his only three-putt of the week. It was the last of 82 strokes on his beloved playground, the highest score he had ever shot in the Open. His 155 total was six strokes off the cut. His goal of playing all four rounds in each major would go unrealized.

It was finished. He and Jackie hugged on the green, then Jack greeted Barbara and his other sons, Steve, Gary, and Michael, with more hugs and tears.

"I love you," Barbara said, her eyes red from crying.

"Well," he said with a shrug and fighting back more tears, "that's the end of it."

⌐

Say it ain't so, Jack.

But it was so. Nicklaus had seen the moment of his greatness flicker.

"I'm ready to let it go," he said with perspective and honesty, "and I'm ready to let it go for a very good reason, and that is that I don't think that I can compete anymore. I have no problem in letting go at all."

Prior to the championship, Nicklaus had talked about how Pebble Beach always responded to his golf game, "or I responded to it." But as the conditions became more difficult that Friday afternoon, his game couldn't keep up, even though he said he had hit the ball "as good as I can hit it." That being the case, and after the struggles he endured at blustery Augusta, he could come to but one conclusion.

"I shot 155 and that means one of (three) things: I don't have the skills around the greens anymore, I don't have the concentration, or I just don't have the golf game anymore.

"I've had a horrible time when I get conditions that get hard and fast, which used to be my favorite conditions. That's when I excelled. I can't make those conditions work."

When the media tongues finally tired some 90 minutes after he had completed play, Nicklaus arose slowly, stiffly, from his easy chair, a throne of sorts to which he would never return. Stragglers bid him farewell before he exited to the rear of the giant media tent. A car was waiting to take him away, but the Golden Bear dawdled.

As it should be for the monarch in the kingdom.

"I wasn't supposed to be leaving this soon," he objected. "With the way I hit it I don't know how I could be leaving."

Asked if he intended to stay the weekend, Nicklaus crinkled his nose and shook his head. "Nah, that's like leaving a fish wrapped in newspaper a couple of days too long."

Nicklaus eased himself into the back seat of the gold Lincoln. "It's time to go," he said with a small sigh. The driver dutifully put the car in gear.

There was nothing more to say.

7

SHADOWS

IN THE CRADLE OF GOLF

"I'm tired of giving it my best and not having it be good enough."

—Jack Nicklaus, 1977 British Open

The Old Course at St. Andrews is a restless place. Within its pastoral boundaries—which at first glance evoke serenity—are angry bounces, uncompromising bunkers and hollows, and dizzying lies. And it is all chapped by temperamental winds, which blow, on average, more than 300 days a year. Golf course architect Pete Dye calls St. Andrews "the hardest place in the world."

The prodigal golfer hasn't a prayer of surviving at golf's recognized birthplace. But Jack Nicklaus, an insightful man, immediately was fascinated by its treacherous properties, and there he thrived, too, winning two of his three British Open crowns in successive visits in 1970 and '78. One didn't have to share this affection, however, to properly negotiate his way around the ancient grounds by the North Sea. Bobby Jones won the British Open at St. Andrews in 1927, but during the third round of the 1921 Open Championship, he marched off in a snit after 11 unsatisfying holes, furiously tearing up his scorecard and "retiring," as they used to say.

A number of years later one of Jones' most fervent admirers, Charlie Nicklaus, would come to share the initial sentiments to which his hero was predisposed. In 1959, while Jack competed in his first Walker Cup at Muirfield to the south, the elder Nicklaus and two friends, Asa Devers and Al Johnson, took the opportunity to sample links golf at St. Andrews. They were dubious of its architectural merits, to say the least.

"My dad didn't think much of St. Andrews at first. I think he was disappointed initially," Nicklaus said, fondly recalling the long ago occasion of listening to the three older men criticize the place. "When they got back they all said it was the worst golf course they've ever played. Then I found out why. My dad three-putted 15 greens, Asa three-putted 14 of them, and Al three-putted 13 greens.

"The first time I saw it was in 1964 and I didn't understand what my dad was talking about. I've never been in awe of any golf course, but I thought St. Andrews was just a wonderful place to play golf and I loved it immediately."

He also has loved to play in the British Open. While the U.S. Open was most important to him, the British Open represented not only the championship of the remainder of the golf world, but also golf on holiday of a sort. Having said that, the Open Championship was perhaps the most difficult of the four majors for Nicklaus to win. A drastic adjustment was required for him to alter his masterly high-flying drives and iron shots to the low, boring shots that are the most conducive to scoring in the windy links conditions.

"My favorite golf tournament to play in has always been the British Open, because it's so different from what we play everyday at home. Having to play those conditions and what they do over there and the uniqueness of it. It's a thrill every time I go over there just to play."

St. Andrews is sacred to many, but no more than to the Golden Bear, who dedicated his 1970 victory there to his late father after he survived a play-off with unlucky Doug Sanders. His win in '78—which, he acknowledged at the time was achieved primarily with his putter—was among his more satisfying, coming three years after his previous major title and a year after he blistered Turnberry with weekend scores of 65-66 only to fall one shot shy of Tom Watson, who countered with 65-65. Nicklaus may never have been in awe of St. Andrews, but he always has been in awe of that universal incorporation of the eccentric course and the ecclesiastical old gray town into one timeless setting. Any tinkering on the grounds whatsoever would be sacrilege in his mind. Naturally, he was mortified upon learning that alterations had been made in preparation for the 129th British Open.

Nearly 200 yards had been added with new tees at the third, sixth, 10th, 13th, 15th, and 16th, stretching the Old Course to a more modern 7,115 yards for the 26th Open staged at St. Andrews. The changes at 15 and 16 were most meaningful, bringing back into play two famous fairway bunkers, the Sutherland at 15 and the Principal's Nose at 16. But with gain there is inevitable loss, and again it was in the manner of charm. The free-flowing course of earlier generations had been lost. Players faced awkward walks backward from some greens to the next teeing area, which Nick Faldo, among others, detested.

However, the more overt and significant permutation was the reconfiguration of most of the 112 bunkers. The newly shaped sod wall faces were practically vertical. In addition, the concave bottoms had been flattened, which enabled balls to run snug up against those walls, leaving unplayable lies. Together these elements conspired to represent a penalty of at least one full stroke and usually more.

Tom Watson called the bunkers "sunken silos." Mark Calcavecchia referred to them as "Jacuzzis." Whatever they were called, they were unspeakably penal.

Nicklaus first heard rumblings of changes to St. Andrews at the Masters, but didn't obtain specifics until the week prior to the championship. His initial reaction: not again. "Why would they want to change it? Good gracious, when Julius Caesar came through they played on the same golf course. Every time we've played an Open on it for however many years. Why do you want to change it?"

Change, of course, occurs at every golf course. Some of it is natural. Trees grow and die. Erosion sculpts and resculpts the ground. One of the most common changes induced by man is simply stretching layouts to avoid obsolescence.

The St. Andrews of 2000 was to be approximately 800 yards longer than the St. Andrews of Harry Vardon's time 100 years earlier. The course originally was 22 holes, but was trimmed to 18 holes around 1764, establishing what is now the standard. Some of the bunkers have only been in place since around 1900 while a bunker in the shared first and last fairways was removed in 1914. The present-day first green wasn't built until 1870.

But unlike Pebble and Augusta, the changes at St. Andrews did not constitute a vast philosophical departure. Its spirit remained intact.

Funny thing about history: a person's sense of it is strongest in those periods that are personal.

～

Leading up to the British Open, Nicklaus competed in two senior events, both majors, and the best thing that could be said of them was that they developed into minor disappointments, especially considering the serious physical problems that developed during the nearly three-week stretch from June 28 to July 16.

Saucon Valley Country Club in Bethlehem, Pennsylvania, played host to the 21st U.S. Senior Open, an event Nicklaus has won twice to give him eight USGA titles. He entered the event hopeful of creating a dilemma for himself. The winner receives an exemption into the U.S. Open. Though he had just said goodbye to the championship, the thought of earning yet one more berth through his play was appealing.

An opening 4-under-par 67 on Saucon Valley's 6,749-yard Old Course made it a realistic proposition. With birdies on the first three holes, including a chip-in from 25 feet at the third after short conversions at Nos. 1 and 2, Nicklaus enjoyed his best all-around day of golf since his operation. Nicklaus had more control of his golf ball after making, with Lubin's input, a miniscule swing adjustment. He took the club back lower and slower. The tempo was familiar. Nicklaus felt it. Others recognized it.

"It was like the old days. He had that competitive look in his eyes that I always liked. You could see the confidence in his mind," said playing partner Graham Marsh.

"There comes a time when you have to let it go and just play golf," Nicklaus, in sixth place and three behind Bruce Fleisher's record-setting 64, explained. "It was kind of neat. I feel good about the day, but it was just one day."

It was just one day. In Round 2 Nicklaus hit nine fairways, 14 greens and shot a bewildering 75 that included 35 putts. His disgust reached new levels. "It is incomprehensible what is happening with my golf," he said while flipping his shoes dejectedly, end over end, into his locker. "I can't tell you how frustrated I am. It's really eating at me."

Similar results ensued in the third round but a nearly calamitous development overshadowed it all.

Nicklaus stood even par for the day and the championship when he drove into the right rough at the par-5 sixth hole. The ball burrowed to the bottom of the 3½-inch rye, and he was left with no other choice except a hack out to the fairway. The ball popped out hot when Nicklaus hit down on it with his wedge, but the leaves of grass wouldn't give. Nicklaus immediately doubled over in pain. He had pulled a muscle in his upper right ribcage.

Amazingly, his next swing, one-armed with a wedge, checked up seven feet from the flagstick. He missed it. He made several more one-armed passes until a dose of Advil kicked in, but, wincing on every stroke, he couldn't make more than a half- to three-quarters swing. Nevertheless, he set himself up for a half dozen birdie chances inside 20 feet and converted none. It was a brave round of golf. Gutsy. He should have felt proud. But the Advil couldn't dull the ache of a 73.

He should have withdrawn (he has pulled out of only three tournaments in his career because of injury), and later he learned that a full recovery would take six weeks—with complete rest. Instead, Nicklaus gutted out a phenomenal 1-under 70 in the final round and finished at 285, good for 21st place, his highest in 10 Senior Opens. Playing partner David Graham joined the gallery in rapturous applause for Nicklaus after he closed with a 12-foot par putt.

Later that day Hale Irwin, after a second straight 65, joined Nicklaus, Gary Player and Miller Barber as multiple U.S. Senior Open champions. Irwin, a three-time U.S. Open champion, completed 72 holes in a record 267, three better than Fleisher, and with his 28th win edged within one victory of Lee Trevino's all-time Senior PGA Tour mark.

⌐⊃

Nicklaus' ribs were only marginally improved when he teed it up July 13 in the Ford Senior Players Championship in Dearborn, Michigan, the year's final senior major. But compounding Nicklaus' woes were the lingering effects of an intestinal infection that had sent him to the emergency room six days earlier. Antibiotics cured him sufficiently but zapped him of strength.

"I get sick for trying to get well," he said with bemusement.

Nicklaus, who won the event in 1990 and never finished out of the top 25, opened with a 75 after a 2-under start through six holes on the 6,966-yard TPC of Michigan course he designed. He followed with rounds of 72 and 71, and played better tee to green each day. But he couldn't shake his putting slump. The ongoing saga of putter tryouts continued between rounds. Three more came and went. During Saturday's round he experimented with eight different strokes, he said, which hardly promotes confidence or consistency.

"Playing golf is putting all the things together. I can hit the golf ball, but it's getting to a number I struggle with. When the day's over it's all about scoring."

With the British Open and the prospect of veritable torture on some of the world's most treacherous putting surfaces closing in, Nicklaus, in need of a quick cure, once more sought the counsel of a trusted peer. Dave Stockton, regarded as one of the game's finest putters, provided a quick lesson prior to the final round. As a remedy for Nicklaus' ailment, primarily his inability to start the ball on line, Stockton suggested putting more weight on the ball of his left foot and dropping his left shoulder.

Improvement was immediate. "All of a sudden my eyes adjusted to what I was doing and the putter blade looked like it was part of me rather than some foreign object. The ball actually was going where I was looking."

While Ray Floyd was shooting a 66-273 and rallying from six back to win for the first time since the '96 Senior Players, Nicklaus was moseying along with a calming 70. He ended up tied for 34th but he made a couple of longish putts, including three birdies from 8, 10 and 20 feet at the 15th, 17th, and 18th, respectively, to fight back to even-par 288 for the championship. He was so pleased with the results that he passed along the tips to playing partner John Morgan as they walked off the final green. Nicklaus even gave a brief demonstration greenside. He was smiling, perhaps as much in relief as happiness—and with good reason. As he himself wrote in his book, *My Story*, putting would be crucial. "Although every golf tournament is to some degree a putting contest, the premium on the short stick at St. Andrews is greater than anywhere else in the championship game."

Those hard, crusty, and wildly undulating greens by the Firth of Forth didn't seem so ominous anymore. "I feel like I at least have a chance to play well now," was the last thing he said before embarking across the Atlantic Ocean.

⌒

For a man with a balky putter, St. Andrews, circa 2000, was a chamber of horrors. Practically the whole yard was a putting green. The fairways looked like they had been shaved within an inch of their lives and were as forgiving as granite—the better to serve as runways to terminal lies in those penal bunkers. A dry Scottish summer stretched into championship week, exacerbating the fast conditions. The gigantic double greens that serve 14 of the 18 holes were slick, short, and swift.

This is what greeted Jack Nicklaus when he arrived in the Kingdom of Fife for his seventh Open at St. Andrews.

A man afraid of heights might have felt more comfortable climbing Mount Everest.

The first two days of practice Nicklaus adjusted to the time change and course changes—he described the bunkers as "by any stretch of the imagination the most difficult situation I've ever seen,"—and locked in on a swing that would be serviceable. He also failed to one-putt a single green or register one birdie.

So much for putting tips.

Nicklaus practices as hard as he plays so he could not feign ambivalence. He was irked. "I have been putting atrociously," he groaned. "It's not been particularly fun."

His mood lightened on the eve of the championship, his ninth straight day playing golf, despite the fact it was one of the longer days he ever spent on the course prior to a major. Another millennium Open meant more pomp and circumstance. But unlike the U.S. Open, where the past champions merely were feted, R&A officials asked former British Open winners to participate in a four-hole exhibition covering holes 1, 2, 17, and 18. The Past Champions Challenge, thought up by Lee Trevino, wasn't a terribly huge imposition, but it altered routines and kept a handful of tournament competitors out in the broiling sun for an extra hour or more.

Nicklaus, nevertheless, chose to play 18 holes before the exhibition. John Daly, fellow senior tour player Christy O'Connor Jr., and 21-year-old Walker Cup player Philip Rowe of England joined him. Daly, 34, who won the '95 Open at St. Andrews, holds a special reverence for Nicklaus and couldn't have been happier to tag along.

"Are you kidding? It was a very special day," Daly would say later. "No matter who you are, something like that is a memory as long as you live."

There were many memories from this day as 22 former Open champions—including 88-year-old Sam Snead, who had not been back to St. Andrews since his win in '46—participated in the exhibition, which began at 4:40 p.m. local time. The threesome of Tom Weiskopf, Tom Lehman, and defending champion Paul Lawrie were the victors at 2 under par in the better-ball format, but the golf hardly mattered.

Snead, a charming presence as well as an inspiration, teed the ball up for his second shot to 17. As he crossed the Swilken Burn Bridge, Snead performed a brief soft-shoe dance. On the same hole, Nick Faldo buried his approach into the Road Bunker and escaped by throwing the ball onto the green. Ian Baker-Finch hit his opening tee shot out-of-bounds right, making him the first man to miss the widest fairway in the world on either side. (He hooked it left across the adjoining 18th fairway in '95.) Justin Leonard, at 28 the youngest of the former winners, donned a white shirt and necktie, while Gary Player wore the same two-tone trousers, one pant leg black and the other white, he had first worn in 1960.

Argentine legend Roberto de Vicenzo, 77, paired with Nicklaus and Tom Watson, nearly drove the 357-yard par-4 18th with the aid of a noticeable tailwind, the first stirrings from the normally busy breezes. Nicklaus, his rib injury close to a nonfactor in the warmth, made note of the fresh breath blowing in. Concentrating like always, Nicklaus' philosophy was to have fun while making good use of his time. "It was nice to see a breeze come up," he said, "and figure out a little of what it's going to do to the golf course."

The day's strongest memory for Nicklaus was of a British Open he hadn't even attended.

While completing his practice round with Daly, O'Connor, and Rowe, Nicklaus came upon Frenchman Jean Van de Velde waiting to tee off at 18. Van de Velde had etched his name into Open Championship lore in dubious fashion a year earlier at Carnoustie with a disastrous 72nd hole. Via an incalculably foolish series of shots, he triple-bogeyed out of the Barry Burn on the par-4 hole when a double would have won the title, and he ended up losing a four-hole play-off to Scotland's Lawrie.

"I wish I had been with you at 18 last year. I'd have kicked you right in the ass," Nicklaus told Van de Velde, joking with him while also offering him a modicum of comfort.

"It's only a game," Van de Velde debated.

"I know it's only a game, but you don't get many chances," the Bear admonished.

What he left unspoken was that mere mortals do not get many chances. Legends are another matter. From 1963-80, Nicklaus had a shot at the Claret Jug every year. His worst finish in that span was 12th, in 1965, at Royal Birkdale, and he placed out of the top five only twice. In his 36 previous starts he had only missed four cuts, three of those coming in the mid-'90s.

It is only a game. Nicklaus himself had said that hundreds of times. But he also was of the mindset that if you're going to play, then play to win or don't play at all. He was a 250-1 long shot for the Millennium Open, but that didn't stop him from preserving that mindset. Play to win or don't play at all.

෧

There is no such thing as a casual stroll through a minefield.

Playing in Game 38—or the 38th group—with Argentina's Angel Cabrera and controversial Ryder Cup captain Mark James of England, Nicklaus suffered almost endlessly on the serpentine slopes of the Old Course in his opening round on July 20. He racked up 34 official putts but used his flat stick 39 times in shooting a 5-over 77. Yet once more Nicklaus was perplexed by hard and fast conditions while 80 players, led by Ernie Els with a 65, were beating par on the sunny and slightly breezy day.

Things began ominously with a double-bogey on the benign first hole—only the second time in his career he had opened a major championship in such a poor manner. A good drive left him 91 yards from the flag, but he dumped it in the Swilken Burn that runs in front of the green. The hole is named "Burn" and it scalded the Bear.

He righted himself with a birdie from 16 feet at No. 2, but three-putted the third from 12 feet. He had plenty of time to stew on that one. For the second straight major there was a backup on the fifth hole, this one a par 5 of 568 yards that was easily reachable on the rock carpeting of St. Andrews.

Nicklaus ambled over to where a group of reporters, including his longtime biographer Ken Bowden, had settled in for the wait. The conversation turned to Nicklaus' early golfing years, how he had shot 51 the first time he played nine holes, followed by a 61 and a 71 in successive tries.

"Early signs of choking," he said wryly.

When another writer suggested that Nicklaus hadn't choked on a golf course in his life, he was promptly corrected.

"I just choked on the first hole," Nicklaus asserted. "(The late) Henry Longhurst would have said that I made a dog's meal out of it."

Nicklaus two-putted the fifth from 20 feet for birdie to go out in 37, but his round fell apart at the back end of that famous stretch of cloistered holes, 7-11, known as "The Loop." At No. 10 he three-putted from 50 feet. At the short 11th he used his putter three more times, once from off the green, for another bogey. A third consecutive bogey at 12 was the result of three putts from 35 feet behind the hole. At 14, the only other par 5, two big shots put Nicklaus just in front of the green. But a poor chip caught a slope and careened off the steep side of the putting surface and yet three more putts resulted in another bogey.

The day stacked up like this: 11 fairways, 11 greens, and five three-putts, including a crusher at the 18th. Six times he missed for par within six feet. The dejection was etched on his face as he emerged from the scoring trailer to the right of the first tee. He refused to make any excuses. His ribs hurt, his feet were killing him and he was still mending from that intestinal infection.

Asked if his ribs hindered him, he replied sternly and sullenly: "It's just me. I'm the only thing that's bothering me."

That's all he had to say. Head down, he trudged into the archaic Royal and Ancient clubhouse alone. The weekend already appeared lost, but there was no concession from the Nicklaus camp. "It could still happen for him," Barbara said afterward. "He deserves for something good to happen, for some putts to start dropping. It has to start happening. It just has to."

You could tell she wanted it just as badly as he did.

⌇

Jack and Barbara Nicklaus chose their wedding date, July 23, 1960, simply because it did not conflict with his golf schedule. It was the week of the PGA Championship, which was being held that year at Firestone Country Club in Akron, Ohio. Nicklaus, the reigning U.S. Amateur champion, was not eligible.

They celebrated two anniversaries at the PGA, in 1966 and '67, but after the PGA moved permanently to August in 1972, their special date coincided most often with the British Open. In 2000, as fate would have it, the final round was scheduled for July 23.

Barbara informed Jack that there was no need to shop. "I told Jack all I wanted for an anniversary present is for him to be playing on Sunday. As late as possible, of course, but I'll settle for him playing."

It was a fitting request. The day after their wedding, the newlyweds embarked on a trip to New York City in Jack's white 1959 Buick convertible. They stopped in Hershey, Pennsylvania, and Nicklaus played golf at the country club, which was headed up by Jay Weitzel, a former assistant at Scioto under Jack Grout. Two days later he played Winged Foot in Mamaroneck, New York, in a driving rain. After a short stay in Manhattan, the couple drove south to Atlantic City, but Nicklaus noticed that Clementon, New Jersey, was on the way, sort of. He talked Barbara into stopping at Pine Valley, had the good fortune to run into Dave Newbold, a Philadelphia insurance exec who recognized the Amateur champ, and he played while Newbold drove Barbara around the male-only club's perimeter, where she caught glimpses of his round.

Now if she could just watch him play this weekend.

⌐

Nicklaus spent a quiet but agitated evening Thursday at the Ruflets Hotel, where he and Barbara have stayed since their first visit to St. Andrews in 1964. Nicklaus seldom dwells on his golf once he leaves the course, but Thursday's round troubled him because his competitive performance in no way reflected the extent and quality of his preparation.

"He was so bummed," Barbara said.

But just as he always had before, he reacted with even greater degrees of determination. The depth of his desire and of his affection for the Old Course and this old event spilled out before he even took a swing in Round 2. His eyes misted as he was introduced on the tee. He would not, however, allow his emotions to compromise his concentration as he had in the early and waning moments at Pebble Beach. Soon he had the loyal Scottish patrons crying for more.

On another atypically sunny, warm, and relatively windless day, Nicklaus birdied the first hole with a 40-foot putt and added one-putt pars at two and four and a routine par at the third. Bedlam erupted at the fifth. He smacked his drive 313 yards and ripped a 3-iron onto the front edge of the green. His eagle putt rattled in and out, eliciting a huge groan from the crowd. He tapped in for a birdie to go two under. Then he nailed an 18-footer for a third birdie at the sixth, a 412-yard hole that is the second-longest par 4 on the front nine.

Three under through six holes, Nicklaus was now 2 over for the championship and in position to make the cut.

The crazed fans were ready to explode when the Bear launched a wedge within seven feet of the flagstick at the par-4 seventh. What a script Nicklaus was authoring. "Then I kicked myself in the gut," he said. And once he was wounded, the Old Course did nothing to pick him back up.

Golf courses are long on memory and short on sympathy.

The 7-footer was as basic as they come: straight in, slightly uphill. The thing stayed above ground. "A crusher," Steve called it. "It derailed us and we never got back on track."

Three-putts at the eighth and 12th were further body blows. When he drove into the Beardies, a nasty collection of pot bunkers left of the 14th fairway, another bogey could not be avoided and he could no longer keep his heart aloft. "After that I wanted to get in the house without embarrassing myself."

First there was a bit of orchestrated sentimentality to negotiate. Five years earlier Arnold Palmer had paused on the Swilken Burn Bridge and waved goodbye to the adoring masses as he played the 18th hole in his final British Open. Now it was Nicklaus' turn to cross that storied stone structure that arched over the burn—which to him must have looked like the River Styx—before traipsing through the Valley of Sin.

A fine tee shot preceded the necessary stop on the Bridge. Some 50 photographers materialized seemingly out of the ocean air to capture the moment. Resplendent in tan slacks and a yellow shirt that gleamed in the sunshine, Nicklaus tipped his brown cap to the gallery that had swelled on the adjacent street called Granny Clark's Wynd.

Tears in his eyes now, Nicklaus waved son Steve onto the crest of that bridge for more photos. He greeted him with open arms and patted him on the head.

"Walking over the Swilken Bridge for the last time was very nice," he explained later, "but not on Friday afternoon."

To his left, above the huge grandstand, waved 28 international flags, and they all pointed in the direction of the Bear. As if he needed the extra attention. With thousands of eyes upon him and millions more watching at home (ESPN extended its coverage an hour to capture the closing moments), Nicklaus hit a 9-iron to about six feet, and, with putter in his left hand and his hat in his right, he accepted more applause as he approached the large green. Some in the audience had taken to donning gold T-shirts that read, "Farewell Big Jack."

So many times in his career, no matter what had occurred before, Nicklaus found a way to birdie the final hole. It was a trademark of his. But in a replay of Pebble, the walk off at St. Andrews wasn't quite right. "It broke like the devil," he said of that final, futile distance to be covered. "I wanted to make that putt so badly, and I just hit a terrible putt." It never had a chance of falling and Nicklaus tapped in for a 1-over 73 and 150 total, six shots adrift of the cut.

The putt wouldn't drop, but more tears did. After years of rarely showing emotion, he had in the last two majors spilled a little of himself on "those two shining lights" in his golfing life. In that baptismal process he illuminated the corners of himself. The walk off wasn't bad after all.

He shared an embrace with Steve and blew a kiss to the crowd before his aching feet carried him slowly from the tired turf to the stone steps leading to the R&A clubhouse. As he made his way to the scoring trailer, head down, he did not even notice the young man some 50 yards away preparing for his second round. He did not see Tiger Woods nearby. Woods, eyes fixed down the first fairway, didn't see the Golden Bear, either.

So close, and, yet, they were worlds apart.

But Jack did see Barbara after emerging from the trailer. His eyes immediately turned misty again. She gave him a kiss, and so did his daughter, Nan, who more than her brothers has shared her father's affection for the annual overseas pilgrimage.

"It certainly has been an emotional month," Barbara said as she fought a catch in her throat.

⌇

In the modern sports era, a golfer can encounter a nearly endless stream of interview requests after his round—considerably more than an athlete in any other sport where access is regulated and buffer zones are built in. The process can be exhausting and exasperating, even for that most patient breed of player—the one who has just won a tournament.

For the second consecutive major championship Nicklaus had to suffer not only missing the cut, but also having to relive the nauseating experience over and over. It is questionable whether anyone other than Nicklaus or Arnold Palmer would have endured the chore with as much grace. In fact, Nicklaus had gone through it many times before. The first time he bucked up to face the media in an unpleasant circumstance was after shooting 76-77-153 and missing the cut as defending champion in the 1963 U.S. Open at The Country Club in Brookline, Mass. Adhering to the advice of his father, who taught him that it was his responsibility as a professional athlete to accept the bad with the good, Nicklaus talked with writers at such length and depth that they gave him a standing ovation at the end of the interview session.

There was Charlie Nicklaus' son 37 years later still accepting. Again he put a fine point on where he was finding himself in the game. Moments earlier in the scoring trailer, Nicklaus had barely finished checking off his scorecard when championship committee chairman Hugh Campbell queried whether he might consider a return if the Open were brought back in 2005. Campbell said the championship committee would bring it back "just for him." Touched, Nicklaus said he wouldn't rule it out, but he was not hopeful.

"I never say never, but the chances are not good," he said. "I would say the chances are I've played my last hole in the British Open. The time comes when you just don't put a number on the board anymore."

As he had at Pebble Beach when he spoke of his affinity for the grueling golf of the U.S. Open, Nicklaus took the time to communicate exactly what the British Open has meant to him. "The Open Championship has been a big part of my education and a part of my maturation in golf. And it has been a big part of my life.

"I've had some great memories from here. It has always been my favorite event. It has been a great place to play golf. I think that to come over to the British Open, to take the difference in the golf courses, the difference in the conditions we play…everything is to me going back in time almost. It may sound silly, but in many ways it is."

No one would blame Nicklaus for wanting to reverse the calendar. But no sooner had he completed his discussions with the media, he began contemplating the future.

"OK, what is there to do in London tomorrow?" he said. He didn't really care. His mind was leaping beyond that, to the PGA. He was thinking of how he was going to prepare, what adjustments he would make, how he could improve his chances of playing four rounds.

"Now I have to get you four rounds at Valhalla, Stever. Jackie got six rounds, you deserve six rounds, too.

"The first thing I might do is look at trying some different golf balls," he added. "Just to see."

That decision was cemented three days later when he watched Gary Player clout some prodigious drives with the new Rule 35 ball from Callaway.

Nicklaus was raring to get right back to it, but there was no more golf to play. The only strokes left for him were the countless hundreds with his marker pen. The British masses, eager for a glimpse of their weathered hero, anxiously awaited his appearance. The file of autograph-seekers stretched 100 yards beyond the R&A clubhouse and Nicklaus almost instantly was engulfed by the human gauntlet.

Except for the last hole, Nicklaus didn't see the remainder of the championship. He watched on television from the clubhouse at Sunningdale Golf Club, near London, as Tiger Woods dropped in a 6-foot par putt on the last hole to win by eight strokes with a tournament and Old Course record 19-under 269 total. Thirty years before, Nicklaus had cemented his standing in the game by making an eight-foot birdie putt to defeat Doug Sanders in a play-off for the 1970 Open Championship at St. Andrews. Woods now had done the same, but had gone several better with a second straight annihilation of his peers, a championship record, not to mention the all-time major scoring record, and the completion of the career grand slam. He became the fifth and youngest man to achieve the distinction. The others, in order, were Gene Sarazen, Ben Hogan, Player, and Nicklaus.

Nicklaus left for London late Saturday morning, saw the musical "Chicago," that night at the Adelphi Theatre in the city's West End, and then, of course, played golf Sunday—on his anniversary—to prepare for a match against old foe Gary Player in *Shell's Wonderful World of Golf.* It was hardly a joyful round.

"I don't want to be here," he told Jackie, playing alongside, after five holes of mysterious military golf.

Jackie struck upon an idea. "Dad, you've always played from outside and then underneath your swing plane. Why don't you try to take it outside going back. Be ridiculous with it."

"OK, I'll be ridiculous with it," Jack responded, figuring it couldn't hurt.

It didn't hurt at all. In fact, there was immediate improvement. Within a span of a few holes he could stand confidently on the tee, aim down the left side, and know—just know—that he wasn't going to lose it left. In his prime, that was how he played his most effective golf, by eliminating one side of the golf course.

It was just the tonic to soothe Nicklaus' aching heart.

Monday's *Shell* match, which aired in the fall on ESPN, depended largely on the ability of Nicklaus to rise to the occasion emotionally. Player's gregariousness would emerge regardless of the proceedings on Sunningdale's New Course or the quality of his golf. But that wasn't going to carry a 90-minute program. Nicklaus is more entertaining than the majority of players, but the level of his effort was likely to be proportionate to his level of play.

Player, who also missed the cut in his record 39th Open start, was eating breakfast in Sunningdale's clubhouse by the time Nicklaus arrived. Sunningdale holds a special place in Player's heart; he won his first professional tournament on its Old Course in 1955.

Nicklaus and Player share a strong friendship. Player has been a frequent houseguest throughout the years and Nicklaus named one of his children after his friend. Like Nicklaus, Player isn't one to pull any punches. There are aspects of the modern game that astound him, and he's never at a loss to weigh in. One issue is the amount of prize money available and some players' unwillingness to travel even a little to support some of those events.

"They have a $5 million tournament at the end of the year and you hear some people say they are too tired to play in it," said the noted fitness fanatic, who prides himself on the claim that he is the most traveled golfer in history, with an estimated 10 million miles logged. "When I hear that, I just want to puke."

⌣

Nicklaus, perhaps with Open disappointment still resonating in his restless brain, hit the emotional nail on the head as the pair walked off the first tee just after 1 p.m. Noting that Player was using the new Callaway ERC driver and a Callaway ball, Nicklaus said with half-hearted jest, "New ball, new driver…too bad they can't make a new us."

But the new swing adjustments put a little life in the Bear. He made eagle from 10 feet on the par-5 opening hole and staked himself to a three-shot lead when Player inexplicably three-putted from six feet for a bogey. The Bear also reached the par-5 sixth in two shots and made another birdie to move in front by four strokes.

Player continued to outdrive him, however, a fact that Nicklaus did not fail to bring up time and again. After yet another remark on the subject, Player retorted, "Want to swap scores?"

Player finally birdied the ninth hole with a 20-footer, turning his back and raising his arms before the putt dropped, but the early damage by Nicklaus proved a fait accompli. Nicklaus grew more confident as the round progressed, reached all four of the par-5 holes in two shots on the 6,617-yard layout and wound up shooting 67 to Player's level par 71 for his fifth win in six *Shell* appearances.

"I've always enjoyed these kind of matches; they're a nice change of pace for us," Nicklaus said afterward. "And I certainly enjoyed sharing the day with Gary. We had a lot of fun out there."

Of course he did. Nicklaus had just played a round of golf that had the distinct scent of discovery—or rediscovery. "I was mucho better," he beamed. "I never had one shot that was close to going left today. I missed a few left that went straight, but I got myself in a pattern, which is what I've always done.

"The key is you have to set yourself up in a pattern. I've even done it with my chipping and putting—that's as far as the feel of what to do. I want to feel like I'm almost cutting everything. It's what I've always done to sort of lock in some consistency to what I'm trying to accomplish. It doesn't mean you can't play other shots, but you have to be set in what you're trying to do to allow yourself to get in a position to compete. That's how you play championship golf."

If only he had made this discovery sooner. "That's the way it is. I never look back. Not even a few days. I just don't. Sure, I would like to have found this sooner, but I found it when I found it."

⌐

Afterward, Nicklaus and Player attended dinner with Shell Oil execs and their guests at the quaint Taplow House Inn. A lone bagpiper greeted the party. Dinner included filet mignon. The dessert was a white layer cake with white icing in honor of Jack and Barbara's anniversary.

The evening concluded with the two legends addressing the

dinner audience of about 80 people. They were supposed to make brief remarks, but Player, an incorrigible storyteller, couldn't help himself and rambled on for some 20 minutes. He repeated his favorite story, the one he told in the presence of a mortified Arnold Palmer a few years ago on The Golf Channel's *Golf Talk Live* program. Palmer hates this story.

Some years ago the two men were competing in Japan when, as Player so delicately put it, "Arnold breaks wind." The Japanese officials were furious…at Player.

"Mr. Player, you embarrass us; fart on TV. Very bad," Player said, feigning a Japanese accent. "I tried to tell them it wasn't me, but I'm with the King. I have no chance."

Player laughed heartily with the audience. Then he turned serious.

"Tiger Woods is dominating like no one ever has and he is going to do so much for the game of golf," Player said. "He already is a great player, but I've said before that longevity is the real measure when comparing records, and that man seated right over there is the greatest player the game has ever seen."

When broadcaster Jack Whitaker, who served as dinner emcee, introduced Nicklaus, the Golden Bear arose and said, "Jack, I don't know whether to thank you or shoot you for making me follow Gary Player."

Commencing with his own brand of charm, humor and wit, Nicklaus spoke often of competition and his affinity for it. He closed with a joke:

A fellow owned a dog that liked to watch golf on television, and the pooch leaped head over heels whenever Nicklaus made a par. It flipped twice for birdies. Amazed by the act, a bystander asked the fellow what the dog did when Nicklaus won a tournament. "I don't know," the man replied. "I've only had him for five years."

8
SUNSET

THE GODS AT VALHALLA

"Wait a minute! What's wrong with Valhalla?"

His blue eyes narrowed slightly and a look of disdain washed over his rugged face. Jack Nicklaus was answering a question with a question of his own. He'd been hearing the veiled slights all year, about three regal golf courses in the major championship rota, about revisiting three cathedrals, three courses on which he basked in glorious victory; what a fortuitous convergence. But there are four major championships, and as the year's finale, the 82nd PGA Championship, approached, the veiled slights disappeared. They were replaced by overt slights.

Valhalla Golf Club in Louisville, Kentucky, which was designed by Nicklaus in 1986, paled in comparison to Augusta, Pebble Beach and St. Andrews. It was too new, some said, lacking history. Others claimed it looked too much like a typical PGA Tour stop, lacking aura. It was too soon returned to the schedule, having hosted the 1996 PGA—the quickest return for a major championship since 1910, when the U.S. Open revisited Philadelphia Cricket Club in Chestnut Hill, Pennsylvania, after a three-year hiatus. And, most egregiously, it represented too much of a pure money grab by the PGA, which owns the facility.

However one wanted to view the issue, Valhalla, which means heaven in Norse mythology, was an anomaly. It was no paradise compared to the others. "I don't think you are going to say that Valhalla is in the same caliber as those other three courses," Tiger Woods said diplomatically—much more diplomatically than David

Duval, who a few years earlier said Valhalla, "was a perfectly nice golf course—for a Nike Tour event."

Bob Baptist, who first began covering golf for the *Columbus Dispatch* in 1985, aptly described Valhalla's deviation from the other venues in his tournament preview story, published on August 18, the eve of the championship. Baptist wrote:

> "Jack Nicklaus' final lap in the major championships he dominated in his incomparable career began at Amen Corner in April, continued along the scenic cliffs of Pebble Beach in June, took him across the aged Swilcan Bridge at St. Andrews last month and will end this week under electrical power lines in Kentucky."

So, when a reporter now had the temerity to query Nicklaus about his strong emotional bonds to a certain trio of pre-World War II layouts, the Golden Bear was going to be sure to make his point. At least he was going to try. But soon after his inquiring rebuttal a grin crept into the corners of his mouth.

What's wrong with Valhalla? Nothing that 50 years of history couldn't cure.

Nicklaus closed his eyes and nodded in acceptance. "True," he said after a pause. "It is a little out of sync." So if he had his druthers, would he remain at Valhalla or would he play somewhere else? "That's a good question. Let me think about it."

He began to rattle off alternatives. Baltusrol. Oakland Hills. Firestone. Oakmont. Ah, yes, other fields of conquest. There were so many. Oak Hill, where he won the last of his five PGAs, came to mind. So did Canterbury, where he won his 14th major and passed Bobby Jones. He couldn't omit Scioto, where he grew up with the game. Finally, he struck upon a suitable candidate: Pinehurst No. 2. Carved in the sand hills of North Carolina, Pinehurst, like Scioto, was designed by Donald Ross. Nicklaus won the 1959 North and South Amateur on Pinehurst No. 2. His son Jackie did likewise in '85. Pinehurst, with its small, raised and undulating greens, strategic bunkering and peripheral waste areas, is Nicklaus' favorite golf course from an architecture standpoint.

Soon, however, Nicklaus turned his thoughts back to Valhalla. He understood why it didn't inspire the same respect, but, nevertheless, he was proud that one of his golf courses once again was hosting a major—perhaps his last major.

"It's a nice place for me to finish," he said, inadvertently dropping a hint. "I'm happy it's Valhalla. That means a lot to me. It keeps it personal."

Which, in that regard, made it a perfect fit.

⌐

Before playing another round of tournament golf following his *Shell* game in England, Nicklaus changed roles and served as caddie in a one-day tournament on July 29 near his home in Jupiter, Florida. The fact that it was a junior tournament covering seven holes did not mean he wasn't going to take it seriously.

Jack's seven-year-old grandson, Nick, called on the telephone and asked him if he was free for bag duty. Peepaw, as the grandchildren call him, was delighted to accept. Another grandson, Christopher, after missing out on a shot at No. 1, went for 1-A and asked Barbara to help. A third, Billy, settled for his father, Bill O'Leary, Nan's husband, who is a design associate and vice president for Nicklaus Design.

Christopher, the youngest of the trio, shot a 37 followed by Nick's 38 and Billy's 39. Barbara snickered as she recounted the post-round review with her husband. "He'd have won if he had listened to his caddie," Jack, ever the competitor, informed her.

Such an occasion was a happy reminder why he had undergone hip replacement surgery. It was for quality for life. This was quality time.

⌐

Nellie Helen Nicklaus' quality of life began to dwindle the day 30 years ago when her husband, Charlie, died. She was ready to follow him right then and there, except that she adored her two children, Jack and Marilyn, and their growing families. So she decided that if she couldn't be with the man she worshipped she was going to live to the fullest extent.

The year she decided that she had had enough, that she missed Charlie too much to go on, Helen asked Marilyn to take her back to the Masters, where she hadn't visited since 1963 when Jack won his first green jacket. Now it was time to see one more. That was in 1986. A cherished Nicklaus photo was taken outside the elegant Augusta clubhouse after that tournament. It captures Jack, beaming in his green jacket, sandwiched between his mother and sister, an arm around each of them. (And check out the split in his lower lip.)

But Helen Nicklaus, tougher than frozen asphalt, kept hanging around. Serious health problems first developed in 1988 and in succeeding years she fought off a series of grim maladies. Her doctor, Jim Ryan, first proffered a theory about Helen's unparalleled view of heaven and earth, and his words became the family mantra whenever they contemplated the plight of their matriarch: "She's ready to die, just not right now."

She proved that in 1999 by emerging four times from the clutches of death—her own private grand slam. The drill was always the same. Marilyn would put the call in to Jack and he would rush to Columbus, where he would find her not only alive, but also looking relatively well. She was doing a terrific job fooling everyone, especially her son.

"She was very tough and when she knew Jack was coming, she would rally for him," Barbara explained. "He didn't understand. He would get there and find she was OK. But each time it took a little more out of her."

She rallied one final time for her son's Honoree ceremonies at the Memorial Tournament, and even had dinner at his Muirfield Village home, located off the ninth tee, on Sunday night, May 28, prior to the weather-delayed completion of the tournament. That was the last time she left her home at the First Community Village in Upper Arlington.

By August, Helen, nearing 91 years old, in her mind was still working out the compromise between staying and leaving, but her body independently was moving toward the finish line. Her heart and kidneys were working at about 10 percent capacity. She no longer could fool her son. Nicklaus flew to Columbus on August 5 to attend the wedding of his youngest niece, Katie Hutchinson. The ceremony was held in the Memorial Park at Muirfield Village Golf Club. Because of their pride in Muirfield Village, Jack and Barbara enjoy it when the club is asked to host functions unrelated to golf. One year, classmates from Upper Arlington High School approached Jack about Muirfield hosting a class reunion. Nicklaus gladly obliged, even after he was informed that the dates coincided with the British Open.

He also visited his mother, and he saw for himself that she was failing. He spent an hour with her, and as she had done the last few years, she again expressed her biggest fear, that she would die during an important time in her son's life, during a major championship. She always sacrificed for her children, for their lives, and that wasn't going to change with her dying. She made Jack promise to continue on with whatever he was doing.

⌐

Reluctantly, Nicklaus departed for Portland, Oregon, on Monday, August 7. He was headed to the Fred Meyer Challenge, where he would join son Gary in a team charity event hosted by Peter Jacobsen. Then he was to compete in the AT&T Canada Senior Open in Winnipeg.

Though his mother's health weighed heavily on his mind, Nicklaus looked forward to hooking up again with Gary and taking cuts when it counted, even in an unofficial event. He had managed to get in nine holes at Muirfield Village Saturday and Sunday, but it wasn't productive. He merely had gone through the motions.

"I know I didn't break 40 either time—and I was giving myself some shots. I am the worst recreational golfer in history," Nicklaus declared, perhaps trying not to think ahead to the golf that awaits him if and when he does retire. "Just beating a golf ball around, I have no interest in that. I can't break 90 when I do that. I'm atrocious."

As always, however, one of his boys was going to give him a boost. "I always enjoy playing golf with all my sons," he said. Perhaps part of the enjoyment is a product of the fact that it does him good. On June 20, two days after the U.S. Open, Jack joined his youngest son, Michael, in The Champions Challenge, Johnny Miller's charity event in Lehi, Utah. Playing a scramble format, the two Bears combined for a 12-under-par 60 at Thanksgiving Point Club. They lost in a one-hole play-off to Dave Stockton and his son, Dave Jr.

So Jack was up for a reunion with Gary and what it could do for his spirits. What's more, he hoped to reciprocate by giving Gary a lift. Since his second-place finish at Atlanta, Gary had missed eight of 11 cuts. His best finish was a tie for 25th at the Memorial, which was probably the toughest of them, given the distractions. He was now 89th on the money list, a drop of 50 spots since Atlanta. Nicklaus said he was eager to work with his son to help him get ready for a fall push that would lift him into the top 70 on the money list, a coveted position that meant berths in a number of high-profile events the following year, including The Players Championship, Colonial, and Memorial.

The Nicklauses fed off each other nicely over the two-day, better-ball tournament at the Reserve Vineyards and Golf Club, in Aloha, Oregon. Gary carried the team early the first round and the pair scored a 7-under-par 65. In Round 2, playing with Jacobsen and Palmer, Jack caught fire. He made seven birdies on his own ball as the pair shot 61. They ended up third and split $100,000 as John Cook and Mark O'Meara defeated David Frost and Jim Furyk in a play-off.

Nicklaus made a slight adjustment to his putting crouch at the Fred Meyer, incorporating Stockton's tip of leaning more to his left but pushing his hips forward to allow him to get behind the ball and stroke through it rather than to it. That was the setup he employed in his younger days when his hip could accommodate it. He hadn't been able to copy it for a number of years. Perhaps he was close to copying the results of 20 years earlier.

"Sooner or later they have to start going in," he insisted.

‿

For much of the year Nicklaus had the Sprint International in Castle Rock, Colorado, on his schedule. Slated for the first week in August, the Sprint was on his radar because it is held annually at Castle Pines Golf Club, a Nicklaus layout. It also was a likely place for Nicklaus to join up with his son. The Sprint features the modified Stableford scoring system, which counts points instead of strokes. It is one of two official PGA Tour events not contested at stroke play. The other is the World Golf Championship match play tournament.

Because pars have no point value and the maximum a player can lose on any one hole is three points, for a double bogey (as opposed to scoring two points for a birdie and five for an eagle), the Sprint International promotes aggressive play and is always a shootout. His struggle to convert birdies was reason enough for Nicklaus to take a pass, but the difficult walk at the high-altitude course filled with dramatic elevation changes eliminated any shred of doubt about competing there.

Nicklaus, for all his world travels, had never been to Winnipeg, Manitoba, where the AT&T Canada Senior Open was to be played August 10-13 at St. Charles Country Club. St. Charles is the only course that claims famed architects Donald Ross and Alister MacKenzie as codesigners, with each laying out nine holes at the 27-hole club.

The tournament appealed to Nicklaus for several reasons: because he was guaranteed 72 holes before the PGA, he had the option to ride a cart if his foot pain persisted (he ended up walking all four days), and because he found it intriguing to compete for the Canadian senior crown—having never won the Canadian Open, the only significant championship to elude him.

"I couldn't win the Canadian Open. Maybe I can win the Senior Open," mused Nicklaus, who finished runner-up in the Canadian Open seven times in 25 starts, both records. "But it's been so long since I've been in contention in anything that I get nervous these days playing with my kids."

Being in contention was not just realistic, but somewhat expected. Nicklaus, who decided to put the new Callaway ball to the test in competition, firmly believed his game was rounding into form. "I think

I'm finally getting back to it," he proclaimed at a pretournament media gathering. "I find something new in my golf game everyday. It's coming together and I'm looking forward to putting it to the test in competition."

To prove the point he shot a 3-under-par 69 in the pro-am on four hours of sleep. (After Tuesday's conclusion at Fred Meyer, Nicklaus detoured to California for a site visit to Mayacama Golf Club in Santa Rosa, and didn't arrive in Winnipeg until 2:30 a.m. Wednesday.) When the gun went off in the first round, Nicklaus shot a 4-under 68. He converted five birdies, even making a couple of putts in the 20-foot range, against one bogey, which came at the 17th hole after his approach found a bunker. That bogey stuck in his craw. He had been complaining to Barbara about his inability to finish off a round.

Nevertheless, it was a relatively stress-free round on the tight and short (6,663 yards) course. Nicklaus stood in seventh place, his best position out of the blocks all year.

"I should have gone lower, but I had what I had," said the Bear, sounding like Yogi Berra. "I had an opportunity to shoot really low, but I can't complain. I haven't had many good rounds lately."

Nicklaus was relieved to return to his downtown hotel after a short range session. The crowd at St. Charles was large for a weekday at a senior event in Canada. More than 15,000 people—twice the number organizers expected—passed through the gates, and they were primarily on hand to see the Golden Bear, who first competed in Canada at the 1960 America's Cup Matches and who had been enshrined in the Canadian Golf Hall of Fame in 1995. He was worn out.

But he perked up immediately after receiving a phone call from Scott Tolley. "I hate to be the bearer of bad news," Tolley said, tongue-in-cheek, as a preamble to informing his boss he would be paired with Tiger Woods in the opening two rounds of the PGA Championship. The PGA of America had eschewed the traditional pairing of the last three PGA champions in favor of an elite grouping that also included Vijay Singh, the reigning Masters champion and '98 PGA winner.

Nicklaus, though, knew it wasn't bad news. Publicly, he had fun at his own expense, saying, "Tiger and Vijay are going to be getting their pro-am in after all," and, "I just hope I can stay out of their way." He was reminded of the 1971 PGA. Nicklaus, 31, was paired with Gene Sarazen, who was just days shy of his 69th birthday. The Bear remembered what a thrill that had been. Privately, he was relishing the opportunity to play with Woods. He thought it an honor. More, he was feeling up to the task. His swing was coming around and his foot, thanks to a new insole, had stopped hurting. "Good," he said to Barbara, flashing a mischievous smile and shades of that Nicklaus bravado, "it's about time the kid had some competition."

He certainly was feeling better—more like himself.

⌐

Nicklaus' game held up relatively well for the remainder of the tournament, but it never coalesced as he hoped it would and the Callaway ball experiment came and went without convincing him to make a permanent commitment. He decided he would switch back to his Maxfli Revolution at the PGA.

During a windy second round, which was suspended for three hours by heavy rains (the bad weather seemed to follow him from town to town), Nicklaus hit only three fairways at St. Charles to shoot 73. But once again his putting was more at fault than any other component of his game.

"I had so many putts—easy putts—with an opportunity to get the ball in the hole," he said dejectedly after slipping five shots off the pace. "I fell back into a pattern I've had all year, which is I can't seem to jump on top of a round or hold onto a round when I'm having a little bit of trouble.

"You just have to make your share. I don't want more than my share; I just want my share."

He couldn't help but wonder: how could this possibly keep happening?

In Round 3 he shot 70 with three birdies on the back nine and moved up to a tie for eighth, remaining five shots back. At least he was in contention, which provided a much needed lift. "Who me?" he said, feigning surprise when asked about it. "It's what I came here for." But more important was what he found on the driving range after the round: his old golf swing, or at least a reasonable facsimile. He applied the final piece to the puzzle when he realized he was raising his upper body on his takeaway. Scott Lubin had mentioned it on more than one occasion, as had Jackie, but Nicklaus thought the fault was coming at the top of the backswing, not at the start. The adjustment made his swing clean and tight. He was spanking the back of the ball because he was staying with it.

"I finally figured out what you and Jackie have been trying to tell me," he said to Lubin. "It's what I've been looking for. It only took all year. I'll bet I can even get the ball (high) in the air from this position."

Sure enough, his drives flew a bit higher and a bit straighter with a hint of a fade. Nicklaus had a gleam in his eyes.

It was no surprise he produced his finest ball striking of the year in the final round. What was a surprise, even to him, was that he could muster no better than an even par 72 on a pleasant afternoon void of all but a hint of a breeze. With a 283 total he tied for 14th, nine shots adrift of winner Tom Jenkins. Nicklaus earned $26,100, but little satisfaction.

"Scoring-wise, I just wasn't there," he said with a trace of exasperation. "I don't know why. My scoring ability has been terrible all year."

Returning to Columbus from Winnipeg on Air Bear, Nicklaus didn't dwell on the problem. He played gin with Barbara and studied an atlas. "Can you name the states that border Minnesota?" he quizzed his wife. She shot him a puzzled look.

"Hey, it's the only way to learn," he reasoned. "It's never too late to learn."

It was nearing that point with his golf game, however. "Maybe I'm just putting too much pressure on myself," he speculated. "I've wanted so much to play well this year. I've put pressure on myself my whole career. When I've done that I've always found a way to respond. But it just hasn't happened.

"What the heck," he added blithely. "It's only a silly game."

He was right. There were more pressing matters to contemplate. Before landing in Columbus, he phoned his mother.

⌒

Nicklaus began PGA championship week by visiting his mom. She was in terrible pain and had been put on morphine. Her mind was sharp, but she was barely able to see or hear. She was as light as a feather and Jack choked back tears when he picked her up and carried her from her bed to a couch.

"She was all bones," he said. "Everything hurt her."

But again she mouthed the selfless words to him: "If I die this week, please play. This is a big week; I don't want to mess up your week."

Nicklaus left for Louisville on Tuesday morning with a sense of the inevitable.

The following morning, at about 10:30, Barbara Nicklaus' cell phone rang. She was just leaving a wedding shower for Tabitha Skartved, a Columbus native engaged to PGA Tour player Jim Furyk. (The couple met at the Memorial Tournament a few years ago.) Barbara almost never takes her cell phone with her, much less leave it on. Marilyn was on the other end, saying, "She tried, but she didn't quite make it."

Nearly 30 years after her beloved husband, Charlie, departed, Nellie Helen Nicklaus finally made it a twosome.

Barbara called Tolley, who phoned Valhalla Golf Club. An official from the PGA caught up with Jack on the fourth hole of his practice round and informed him that he needed to call his wife. Nicklaus borrowed a cell phone from his son, Steve, and before Barbara could get a word out, Jack said, "Am I right?"

The color ran from his face when she confirmed the news, but so he would not create a stir, he completed nine holes with Glen Day. He must have signed 100 autographs while walking up the steep hill from the ninth green to the clubhouse.

He knew it was a blessing, and he felt a sense of relief for her, but he struggled to collect himself. He withdrew from Doral when his father passed away. He wanted to pull out now. Barbara and Marilyn dissuaded him; there was nothing he could do. Marilyn would handle the arrangements. They reminded him of his mother's wish.

The funeral was scheduled for Monday in Columbus, on Nellie Helen's 91st birthday.

Nicklaus spent the remainder of the day in his room at the Holiday Inn Hurstbourne, attempting to pull himself together for a dinner that night in his honor at the Kentucky Derby Museum, where he was to receive the PGA of America's Distinguished Service Award. He tried to nap, but couldn't. With the help of Scott Tolley he reworked a portion of his acceptance speech.

When he arrived at the museum, one of the first people to seek him out was Tom Watson. Nicklaus had offered words of comfort to Watson when Watson's father died of a heart attack in January on the eve of the MasterCard Championship. Now Watson wanted to be there for Nicklaus. Greg and Laura Norman also came to give their condolences. So did Pete and Alice Dye.

Nicklaus managed to gut out a 25-minute speech in front of about 1,200 guests. He spoke of his past involvement with the PGA and his five wins in the PGA Championship, from his '63 triumph at sweltering Dallas Athletic Club to the record seven-stroke victory at Oak Hill in 1980. He purposely avoided mention of his mom until the close. He got there by way of recalling his most memorable "shot" in major championship golf—which was taken with a camera and not a golf club. It's a photo of him carrying his four-year-old son Gary off the 18th green after the second round of the 1973 PGA at Canterbury. "The picture brings together in one image my two loves, family and golf," he said.

He paused and cleared his throat. "I'm going to have trouble now."

Nicklaus explained that his mother had passed away earlier in the day, but that he intended to remain. He would be on the tee at 9:13 a.m. with Woods and Singh—and his mom, too. This is how she would have wanted it.

"I'd much rather go, but I'll stay for her. I'll have her in my thoughts and maybe that will inspire me to play a little bit better than I can play.

"It will be a big day for both of us," he managed to eke out before leaving the podium.

⌐⌐

Thursday dawned sunny and hot. By 9 a.m. the humidity was soaking the shirts of the players warming up on the driving range behind the first tee. Just before her husband made his way to the tee box, Barbara stopped Jack and shared a thought for the day. She wanted to lighten the load for him. And she wanted him to focus.

"Just remember," she whispered, "Bears do eat Tigers."

On the tee box Nicklaus took a place between Singh and Woods for a photograph. The two men, each 6 feet 2, towered over the Golden Bear, yet Nicklaus loomed largest with the enormous crowd that had gathered to watch greatness collide. Singh was first in the order and Woods second. When Nicklaus at last teed off and sent his 3-wood shot neatly down the right-center of the fairway just behind Woods' ball, the roar from the gallery standing 6-8 deep on the 446-yard opening hole was like an explosion.

As the three men made their way through the phalanx—a human corridor that would greet them on each hole—Nicklaus couldn't ignore the decibel level. All the screaming and shouting created not just a wall around the players, but also a ceiling over them.

"Is it loud out here or what?" Nicklaus said, turning to Woods.

Woods nodded.

"Thank God I'm done playing," Nicklaus added. "You've got to deal with this for the rest of your career."

Woods was accustomed to the dissonance, but it was different this day. Most of the shouts and cheers were for the Golden Bear. For the first time since he turned professional in 1996, Woods enjoyed a round in the shadows—or at least in one long shadow.

"Today was a great day for me," Woods said afterward. "Everybody was yelling out, 'Jack!' No one saw me. It was kind of nice."

No matter how loudly they cheered, however, they couldn't lift Nicklaus' heavy heart, or his game, to the challenge of his own 7,167-

yard layout. After that perfect opening drive to the right-center of the fairway, Nicklaus badly pulled his 5-iron approach. It landed on a slope left of the green and bounded through a shaved chipping area into a downhill lie in the heavy bluegrass rough.

"Nice kick," he muttered glumly to Steve as he arrived at the ball. He had no shot. His first chip came up short of the green. His second stopped 20 feet shy of the hole. Two putts later he had begun his second straight major championship with a double-bogey—after having done it only once in his previous 157 majors.

Nicklaus followed with bogeys at the fourth and fifth holes after missing the fairways and there was no mistaking that an already difficult day was going to be torture.

"I had no desire to be here, I promise you," he said after the round.

Somehow, though his swing was discombobulated, he managed to sweat through the last 14 holes in one over par, using a series of unlikely saves, including one at the 17th from high grass above a rock outcropping 30 yards left of the putting surface—a place where he never dreamed any ball could end up, let alone his own.

There were a few welcome light moments. At the 166-yard, par-3 eighth, Woods chose a 9-iron that landed 10 feet short of the flagstick. Nicklaus played to the same area and nudged Woods' ball with his own. The Bear had hit a 6-iron. He urged Woods, seated on a bench behind the tee, to turn his club upside down, "so it looks like we're playing the same club."

At the 12th Nicklaus lined up a short par putt, only to have to back away because of a butterfly on the ball. "This has to be some kind of conspiracy," he bellowed.

Fans stood and cheered Nicklaus every painful step of the way, but the best he could do was 77. He said it felt like a 95, mostly because Tiger Woods was systematically constructing a nearly flawless 6-under-par 66 to share the first-round lead with unheralded Scott Dunlap. As they walked off the 18th green, Nicklaus threw an arm around Woods and asked playfully, "What did ya nip me by, 11?"

Nicklaus naturally was discouraged, but Woods' performance oddly provided him a measure of solace. The defending champ put on a display of golf that Nicklaus, above all other witnesses, could truly appreciate. He had, after all, been there and lived it so many times himself.

"That was a real treat to watch today," Nicklaus said. "Phenomenal control. Phenomenal concentration. Getting a chance to watch Tiger in the prime of his career in competition, it was something I have wanted to do."

Somewhat surprisingly, amazement accompanied that appreciation. "He hits his iron shots so far. Gosh, he hits the ball a long way. I couldn't believe some of the places he hit it. And some of the clubs he hit, I never dreamed of hitting those kinds of irons. We're playing the same game, but we weren't playing the same game today."

He couldn't resist recalling Bobby Jones' comment about him after his record-setting 1965 Masters victory. "He plays a game which I am not familiar with," Nicklaus said of Woods. "Of course, I played a game which I was not familiar with either."

Somewhere, Charlie Nicklaus was smiling.

Woods, in the lead for the eighth time in the last nine major championship rounds—Nicklausian dominance—had mutual feelings about the day. "It's special to be able to play with Jack in possibly his last major or even his last PGA," he said. "It's quite an honor to play with him in a major championship."

Equally, Woods admired Nicklaus' style of play, labored as it may have been.

"You can see how he wants to play, where he is lined up, where he is looking in the air, the club he pulls, what kind of shot he wants to play, where he wants to play it," Woods said with a bit of wonder in his voice. "I feel like I have an understanding of how he plays. I kind of play the same way he used to."

Very much so, in fact. It just so happens that when Nicklaus opened the course in 1986, he christened it with a 66.

Once he had completed more than an hour of interviews after the opening round, Nicklaus got on his plane for the 35-minute flight back to Columbus to be with his sister and her family. When the wheels touched down at Ohio State's Don Scott Airfield, Jack looked across into his wife's eyes and said, "It just hit me that Mom's really gone."

So began that most difficult of comebacks—healing from a loss. To hasten the process and regain a measure of normalcy, Nicklaus followed his heart and his gut and stole away to the expansive driving range at Muirfield Village, the place where the ties of golf and family are unmistakably strong and soothing. For an hour just before nightfall, he beat balls in solitude and in the process found solace. He also found his golf swing. His problem, again, was the familiar fault of coming into the ball too steeply. He fixed it before he sat down to dinner at his sister's house.

He, Barbara, and Steve returned to Louisville in the morning, accompanied by Marilyn and her husband, Howard. Awakening in Columbus, Nicklaus had not been aware of a weather delay, and again it had not worked in his favor. The course was softer and the greens more receptive in the morning. Early starters found Valhalla defenseless—heavenly even. If enough players took advantage it could definitely impact the cut.

As usual, Nicklaus wasn't dwelling so much on the cut as on the big picture. Where was he in relation to the leaders? He knew only too well.

When Nicklaus, Woods, and Singh began their second round at 2:25 p.m. Friday, an hour late due to overnight rains, another 66 appeared likely. Early on, it looked like Nicklaus was going to be the one to shoot it.

In a complete turnaround from the previous day, he birdied the first hole after knocking his 5-iron stiff from 172 yards out. When the three-footer dropped, Barbara and Marilyn shared a high-five. "I guess we needed you to be here yesterday," Barbara said to her sister-in-law.

Jack wasn't about to get excited, however.

"Nice putt," Woods offered as they walked to the second tee.

"Thanks," Jack said a bit derisively, "now I'm only 10 shots behind you."

At the par-5 second hole, Nicklaus coaxed in a 20-footer. As the ball trickled in, he pumped his arm forward and pointed at the cup, like he was gunning it down. Two birdies in two holes, and the place was jumping. He stood to make it three straight when his 4-iron stopped 10 feet from the hole on the par-3 hole. The gallery was in delirium. They were pining for a rally, to witness more history. The putt just wouldn't drop.

But a 22-foot putt for par did fall on the fourth hole. More bedlam outside the ropes. He knocked in an eight-footer at the seventh and a two-foot par putt at the eighth to remain two under for the day and three over for the championship. Another routine par at the ninth gave him an outward 34. If he could keep this up he would make the cut. If he could coax in another few birdies, well, who knew what could happen?

"We were pretty much right there with the game plan," Steve Nicklaus said.

But who could have guessed that the rally had stalled at the third hole? Who knew the scoring bugaboo was about to hunt him down again? Two big shots and a chip left Nicklaus with an eight-foot birdie putt at 10. He missed it. At the par-3 11th he was in the fringe but just 14 feet away. Again he exhausted two putts to get it in.

When his approach on the 467-yard 12th hole tumbled into the right front bunker, it spelled trouble. The pin was cut close to the bunker. Nicklaus blasted out to 16 feet past the pin and left the par putt just short. Bogey.

At the short 13th hole, where the green is surrounded by water, Woods lasered his approach to 10 feet, but Nicklaus pitched inside him to seven feet. As the gallery rose for a standing ovation, the two men simultaneously reached the footbridge connecting fairway and green. Woods and Nicklaus instinctively slowed to let the other pass, then exchanged gestures of accommodation. But Nicklaus would have none of it and politely shoved Woods in front of him. Just trying to stay out of the way, you know.

Both men missed their putts, but now things were getting serious for the Golden Bear. Time was running out.

His predicament became more serious when he found another bunker and another bogey at the par-3 14th, pushing him back to five over for the championship, level par for the day. When he missed yet another birdie try, this one from 12 feet, he jutted his chin, as if he were trying to swallow a bitter pill. Perhaps he was. The exasperation was etched on his face. CBS on-course announcer Peter Kostis informed Steve at 16 that they needed to birdie two of the last three to ensure making the cut.

Barbara was still hopeful. "It's not over until the fat lady sings and she hasn't even been introduced yet."

With that, her husband crushed a 4-iron that set up another birdie from 30 feet. No good. At the 17th, an uphill par 4 of 422 yards, Nicklaus hit a poor drive that curved weakly into the right rough. He had 183 yards to the hole from a thick lie below his feet, and he couldn't see the green. It was a poor place for anyone to make a par, let alone think about a birdie. Nicklaus grabbed a 5-iron, ripped through the bluegrass, giving no consideration to his still-sore ribs, and heard the roar. The ball stopped 15 feet from the flagstick.

This is where the happy ending begins, yes? This is where the hard work pays off? This is where it had always paid off for Jack Nicklaus in the past. But again, it was not to be. The Nicklaus will simply could not make it happen.

So it came down to the 542-yard par-5 18th hole. If he took no more than three shots there would be a tomorrow. He knew where he stood. So did Tiger Woods.

After their tee shots came to rest yards apart in the fairway, the two made their way for home. Woods turned to Nicklaus and said, "It's been an honor and a privilege to play with you, Jack. I have enjoyed it. Let's just finish off on a correct note."

"You got it. Let's go," Nicklaus said, still wearing the same look of determination with which he began the day.

It was 7:30 p.m. The sun was too swiftly setting.

↪

"If this is really going to be it, then let it be a good one," Barbara Nicklaus almost whispered the wish to herself.

Jack held a sand wedge and the rest of his competitive life in his hands when she said it. He had layed up perfectly with a 3-wood, and now he was waiting for the retinue to still itself so that he could fully apply the residue of his formidable powers to this last task. Was there still something left inside? All year Nicklaus had been asking himself that question and had been chagrined by the reply.

Possessing equal amounts persistence and optimism, he would ask again.

The answer was delivered as the ball reached its apex. The stroke in a light breeze was nearly perfect. As he had planned, the ball landed past the flagstick onto a small ridge and backed up in the direction of its intended final destination. Barbara would later call it the perfect ending, but her husband stripped it down to a stark truth after it had refused to go in, resulting in a 1-under 71 and an early dismissal. "It ranks one shot short of making the cut."

That everyone in the joint knew it did not diminish their appreciation for the shot or the man responsible for it. "I think Mr. Nicklaus has just introduced himself," bellowed Charlie Eskridge, the blue-blazered PGA representative whose job it is to announce members of each group to the gallery at the 18th green.

"You da man, Jack!" some in the overzealous overflow crowd screamed. Others cried, "We love you, Jack!"

Nicklaus, with his hat in his right hand, acknowledged his legions. Behind him on the large scoreboard was a message: "37 Golden Years at the PGA. Thank You Bear."

Among the noisy thousands was Pete Dye, standing on the clubhouse balcony with Herb Kohler. Kohler is the bathroom magnate who commissioned Dye to build him four world-class courses in the tiny communities around Sheboygan, Wisconsin. One of them, Blackwolf Run, hosted the 1998 U.S. Women's Open. Their latest collaboration, Whistling Straits, is the controversial site for the 2004 PGA—controversial in that the PGA had originally awarded it to Valhalla.

Dye couldn't believe that Nicklaus, who played the last 31 holes in even par, was about to miss the cut. He had walked 12 holes with him

Tuesday and watched Nicklaus hit the ball beautifully. "He looked as good as he ever did," Dye said with wonder.

Nicklaus and Dye, a native of Urbana, Ohio, go way back. Like Nicklaus, Dye is a former state high school champion. He once had watched a teenaged Nicklaus play an exhibition with Sam Snead at Urbana Country Club, which Dye's father, Paul, designed in 1923 when the club's founding members couldn't lure Donald Ross to their small, rural southwest Ohio town. Dye likes to call Nicklaus "Curly."

As they walked that day the two men talked mostly about design. Dye introduced Nicklaus formally to the trade when he solicited from Nicklaus a few ideas that were incorporated into The Golf Club in New Albany, Ohio, east of Columbus. That was Dye's first critical success. The two collaborated on a handful of other projects, most notably Harbour Town Golf Links in Hilton Head, South Carolina. Dye also helped Nicklaus select the current site for Muirfield Village Golf Club, and even offered routing suggestions.

Dye saw how Valhalla was getting beat up in the press and he didn't understand it. "It's really a darn good golf course," Dye said while twirling a bucket hat in his hands.

Dye thought it was only right that Nicklaus get the opportunity to play on the weekend after all that had happened. "You bet I was yelling at that damn ball to get in there," Dye said with a trademark smirk of a smile. "Me and the whole world."

Tom Watson was in the players' dining room, sitting on the edge of his chair in front of a television, when Nicklaus loosed his final arrow. He, too, was part of the cheering section. "I was screaming at the TV," Watson said. "It was a typical Nicklausian finish and it was nice to see. But there could have been nothing better than seeing him play the weekend."

"He was as close as he could get without making it," Steve noted. "He was terrific. He hit it too damn good to shoot 71. Too close."

⌐

There was a palpable sense of passage when Woods vaulted into the lead with his birdie putt at 18. It was unmistakable with Nicklaus' small but significant gesture—that resonating thumbs-up. "A changing of the gods," is how Don Markus of the *Baltimore Sun* sized it up.

The change was complete when Nicklaus bumped in his little birdie putt, the 2,304th hole he has played in the PGA Championship, the 10,476th hole in major championship competition. His 71 marked his 223rd subpar round in the majors, about 70 more than anyone else. He shook hands with Woods and Singh. One last time the galvanized gallery let forth the boisterous chants of "Jack, Jack, Jack!"

If it was his last major championship, a birdie was a fitting conclusion. After all, on the first hole of his first grand slam tournament, the 1957 U.S. Open at Inverness, a 17-year-old Jack Nicklaus sank a 35-foot putt for birdie with an unknowing ease that blissfully accompanies youth. So many years later, after experience had inflicted its tireless erosion, he managed to close with one. Perfect symmetry.

For a fleeting moment time compressed itself.

It was 7:38 p.m. Almost twilight.

A last bit of irony worth noting: As if it were destined, Woods went on to win his third straight major championship, a feat that had not been accomplished since Ben Hogan won the Masters, U.S. Open and British Open in 1953. Three wins for Woods—all with scoring records, mind you—while Nicklaus missed three cuts. Time is a vicious betrayer.

But wouldn't you know there would be one more Nicklaus fingerprint on the proceedings. Woods was taken into a play-off by a little-known journeyman named Bob May, a fine player who had held all the junior golf records in Southern California until Woods, as he is apt to do, wiped the slate clean. For the first time, the PGA of America used a three-hole play-off to determine the winner. Woods wiggled free by a stroke in a memorable showdown.

It's a little-known fact but only once before had a tournament used the three-hole play-off system. It was instituted in 1976 at a budding PGA Tour event (and outlawed one year later by commissioner Deane Beman). Roger Maltbie was the victor over Hale Irwin. Maltbie's prize: the first Memorial Tournament trophy.

That's right, Jack Nicklaus thought it up.

9
TWILIGHT
REFLECTIONS ON A LEGEND

"For the retired warrior there are no anxieties, no agonies, no thwarted ambitions, no wretched little jealousies, no bitter regrets. Never again will he toss and tumble, thinking of the match that is before him on the morrow. No black dances of a missed putt from the match that is past will crouch beside his pillow to arouse him at midnight...There will be no penitence for having been cross, for as far as the game is concerned he need never be cross again."

—Bernard Darwin

The Jack Nicklaus Museum sits in a prominent corner of the sprawling Ohio State University campus in Columbus, Ohio, just off of Olentangy River Road, and, like its namesake, serves to bridge the eras. It cozies up on one side to the Woody Hayes Athletic Field, named in honor of another OSU legend and representative of simpler times. On the other side is the ostentatious Schottenstein Center, an ominous structure born of bloated athletic consumption. It seems appropriate that the road connecting the buildings also is named Jack Nicklaus Drive. The road Nicklaus traveled in his career paved the way for generations of golfers and fans alike.

Due to open in June 2001, the Nicklaus Museum covers 54,000 square feet, sufficient flying elbowroom to house the requisite memorabilia and hardware gathered during the grandest individual golfing dynasty to date. Upon seeing the $10 million red brick building in its early stages of construction, Barbara Nicklaus was struck by the immensity of the place, even as it sat overshadowed by its neighbors. "I didn't realize it was going to be this big," she marveled.

Barbara, of all people, should have had a reasonable idea of the space required to house the cachet of hardware her husband has amassed in more than 40 years of a gifted golfing life. But as with most things modern, value is not in the hardware; it's in the software. Jack William Nicklaus possesses extraordinary human circuitry, and as long as he lives he is the curator of the only artifact that matters: himself.

You can collect all the trophies and medals and scorecards, all the film clips and still shots and equipment related to Nicklaus' career and never approach a meaningful understanding of what he is about, what makes him exceptional among all the players who have ever played the game.

So the question becomes, how useful does Jack Nicklaus want to make that museum? How often will he put himself on display in the future?

⌐⌐

In the weeks following the PGA Championship, Nicklaus went on a scheduled hunting trip in Africa with his sons and concentrated on his innumerable course design projects. He did not play much golf. In fact, when he joined representatives of Marsh & McLennan, the presenting sponsor of his Memorial Tournament, for a corporate outing September 19 at Muirfield Village Golf Club, he had played just 27 holes since Valhalla. That included 18 holes at the grand opening of The Club at Porto Cima in Lake of the Ozarks, Missouri, where he made five birdies and shot a 2-under-par 70. That was encouraging, since Nicklaus puts as much effort into an exhibition as he does a tournament round. Still, it was hardly meaningful. He did not play another 18 holes of golf until the November 15 unveiling of The King & The Bear in St. Augustine, Florida. Palmer and Nicklaus, who waived their design fees (each more than $ 1 million), put on a loose exhibition in which many putts were conceded and many insults were traded. Nicklaus playfully hammered his friend unmercifully over his controversial endorsement of the Callaway ERC II driver, which does not conform to the USGA Rules of Golf.

No sooner had the pair sat down for a press conference before their exhibition than Nicklaus remarked, "I want to hear about this new driver."

"I thought that might come up," Palmer said.

Later, after they announced they would compete as teammates in the 2001 Legends of Golf, which was moving to their golf course, Palmer asked, "What kind of clubs are you going to use?"

"Legal ones," Nicklaus jabbed. "And what are you going to use?"

So it went all day. "Did I have the needle out or what?" Nicklaus said later with an almost dastardly smile.

But he also was quick with praise for his codesigner and for the finished product. "It was a lot of fun to work with Arnold. We had a lot of agreements, not a lot of disagreements, and we ended up with a pretty darn good product."

Later in the day, Nicklaus spoke at The First Tee National Association Meeting at the World Golf Village, where he announced his cochair role, with Juli Inkster, for the "More Than a Game" initiative. The goal of the campaign is to raise $50 million in three to five years to support Phase II of The First Tee, a program created to provide affordable access to the game, especially for youngsters. Additionally, the Bear stepped up with a $1 million donation from the Barbara and Jack Nicklaus Junior Golf Endowment Fund. "I don't get involved with things halfway," he explained. Especially when it comes to helping grow the game that gave him so much.

⤺

The "Silly Season" commenced for Nicklaus the day after The King & The Bear opening. He competed in the EMC Golf Skills Challenge then joined son Gary in Greg Norman's Franklin-Templeton Shark Shootout, which had moved to the Great White Course at Doral. In December he had titles to defend. He and Jackie tied for fifth at the Father-Son Challenge. (Gary, a PGA Tour member, was ineligible to return.) At the Hyundai Matches, Nicklaus and Tom Watson remained unbeaten as a team (they are 8-0, including Ryder Cup competition) in repeating as senior champions.

Undoubtedly, made-for-TV golf and the Senior PGA Tour are the predominant forms of competition in his future—though at the start of 2000 that wasn't what he wanted. How much senior golf he plays will depend largely on the quality of the courses and the difficulty of their setups, the same criteria he applied to his schedule in his prime. "I've never been very good at shooting 65 on an easy course," he explained. "I've always been pretty good at shooting 68 on a hard golf course." This fare, basically, is the stock of a ceremonial golfer, a player who has moved on to a new phase of his career.

Nicklaus wouldn't rule out an appearance in the "odd major." He has lifetime exemptions to the Masters and PGA. He can enter the British Open until he is 65. Making the cut in the 2000 Masters and the Memorial Tournament, two events with which he has the strongest emotional bonds, increases the probability of future appearances in each. In fact, he has said he intends to play in the Memorial as long as he is able. But even as late as December 21, in a teleconference call—one year to the date of his "State of the Bear" press conference—Nicklaus would not commit to a return to Augusta.

Like Palmer, Nicklaus feels the pull of the galleries, who want to watch him regardless of what he scores. Barbara feels it, too. "People don't want to let go of Jack."

Nicklaus, however, said he would not allow himself to be swayed by others. "They're not the ones out there trying to do something they can't do anymore."

Basically, there is no divining his direction. Though he remains a staunch proponent of rolling back distances of modern golf balls, he experimented with a number of brands during the last few months of 2000, figuring he better keep up in the technology race. He also worked out diligently, primarily, he insisted, for his well-being. "If golf is a rub off of that, well, I hope it is," he added coyly.

As the 2001 season got underway, Nicklaus continued his daily physical fitness regimen. When he teed it up in the MasterCard

Championship in January, he was 15 pounds lighter, his foot problems apparently had vanished and he was feeling more fit than he had in a decade. After a sluggish start in the event, he fired a three-under-par 69 in the final round, the day he celebrated his 61st birthday, and finished in a tie for 27th. That proved to be the springboard to his play in the Senior Skins Game the following week, where he won 10 of the 18 skins, collected $260,000, only to finish second to Hale Irwin. But it was the way he finished second that once again captured the admiration of the golfing public. His commitment to sportsmanship, to always doing your best, was exemplified on the 18th green, where he faced a 4-foot birdie putt to tie the skin with Gary Player. If he made the putt, the match went to extra holes. If he missed the putt, he would win outright. He drained it and three holes later Irwin made birdie to win $180,000 to leapfrog over Nicklaus for the Skins title. His plans called for him to play a few more senior events and gauge his competency for the Masters. "If I'm playing decent I'll play at Augusta; if my game is not decent then I won't play at Augusta and we'll just see what happens from there."

The only real certainty is that Nicklaus will remain torn for the foreseeable future.

"I have said 100 times I don't know what I'm going to do. I never want to say I won't do something again. Why would I do that? I'll play golf as long as I can enjoy it and be competitive. I think the two of them go hand in hand. As I become less competitive, a lot of enjoyment goes out of it for me."

You cannot begrudge Nicklaus his hedging. All great athletes have hedged, hesitated and even hallucinated when confronted with the demise of their sunlit days. But his reluctance also is born of a Hogan-like affection for the game's fundamental function: hitting the ball. One could see that during any driving range session when the muscles remembered and club met ball with precision. It was during those moments that the years melted and Nicklaus the icon was a kid again, finding simple joy as he did years ago at Scioto Country Club while whistling shots from the glow of his father's car headlights.

There was one such session in 2000 after the third round of the

Ford Senior Players Championship in Dearborn, Michigan. Nicklaus was striping it. Just barely clipping the turf, he hit a dozen 6-irons that collected in an eight-foot circle. A buoyant Nicklaus all but danced on that sore foot of his.

"I do still love hitting golf shots," he shared with a savory edge. "I like it when I can make a good turn with a wide arc and get through the shot. When I'm swinging well I can feel the shot from right here (he stops halfway down, the club at about 8 o'clock) and all the way through the ball. Now that's fun to be able to do that."

At those times Nicklaus looked as good as ever and the prospect of ceasing championship play had to seem remote to him. But the scores would tumble in and turn him inside out, scores that were no less than an affront to his sensibilities. He was left to face the raw confession that the game elicits.

"No one can make a decision for you when you're going to stop playing," Gary Player said. "But there comes a time, no matter who you are when you just have to stop. There comes a time when you can't play anymore and it's a sad feeling. I can tell you, it is sad."

"Maybe he didn't play as well as he'd have liked to, but he still played great in my estimation," said noted golf writer and historian Herbert Warren Wind, who collaborated with Nicklaus in 1969 on the largely autobiographical book, "The Greatest Game of All."

Wind will be 85 in August 2001, and hasn't written a word, he says, in 10 years. But the man who in 1958 coined the term "Amen Corner," in reference to holes 11-13 at Augusta, pays attention. He follows the game and marvels at how well Nicklaus can play it at 60. "He still hits the ball beautifully. He's still the greatest thinker on a golf course, even now. He's a remarkable player."

Wind drew in a breath and held it, indicating a reluctance to speak. Finally he relented. "It's just not in the cards for anyone to hold back time."

⌐

Nicklaus had wondered aloud at the outset of 2000 if he was "on the wrong side of the age curve" in attempting to come back from hip replacement surgery and in rebuilding a golf game virtually from scratch. In the immediate aftermath of the PGA, he could not have been harder on himself. In the presence of Woods he felt "inadequate," which only meant he'd joined the rest of the competitive crowd. For Nicklaus, that was unacceptable because he always had stood apart from the crowd. He eulogized his ability to play golf.

"I would (continue to) play major championship golf if I thought I could play," he insisted. "I think I stretched it this year playing. I don't think my golf game is good enough anymore. If it's not good enough to play then I probably won't play. If I can't play like Jack Nicklaus, then I don't want to play. It doesn't make any difference to me if it's major championship golf or anywhere, but, obviously, when your ability is leaving you then you go do something else."

Nicklaus, at times, showed he could play. But his good golf came sporadically. Simple numbers bear that out. They are a truth unto themselves.

From January to August, the de facto heart of the golf season in which he would log more than 100,000 miles in Air Bear, Nicklaus competed in 15 official tournaments, eight on the PGA Tour and seven on the Senior PGA Tour, as well as two unofficial events, the Senior Skins Game and the Legends of Golf. Only once since 1986, the year he won his sixth Masters, had Nicklaus competed as often. His best finish was a tie for ninth place at the Countrywide Tradition.

On the PGA Tour, in 19 rounds, Nicklaus posted a career-high 74.66 scoring average. On the Senior PGA Tour, where courses are shorter, the greens are slower and the rough is of negligible length, he averaged 71.84 over 25 rounds, which ranked him among the top 50 or so players—hardly acceptable for a man of such ostensibly lofty standards. Across the board his statistics on the senior tour, predictably, were better than his respective regular tour figures, though, his putting averages were nearly identical—1.872 on the Senior PGA Tour vs. 1.843 on the senior tour. His birdie count on the PGA Tour was the most telling number; Nicklaus tallied 39 of them in 342 holes, an austere 1.84 average per 18 holes.

It didn't help that he never really enjoyed a stretch of good health. He had said from the outset that his success was predicated largely on his health. "Carnac," as his friends call him, got it right. New maladies emerged almost daily—hand, knee, ribs, back, neck—while the pain in his right foot remained a constant. The first week in November he had a cortisone shot for his right shoulder, which he injured two years ago playing tennis. It was always something.

"I'm quickly running out of things to put on the list," he noted with a bit of a laugh.

But there could have been a no more debilitating ailment for his game than his foot problems.

"I've always played golf with my feet. It's one of the major parts of my game as I learned it from Jack Grout," Nicklaus explained. "Whatever I found in my golf game had no chance of lasting because my feet weren't right.

"Unfortunately, the compensation of my left leg for so many years took its toll on my right foot. I didn't have any push off it, no explosiveness. I did not expect that at all. I expected all the exercise I was doing this last year and all the preparation to physically get myself ready to play golf I would get rewarded for, but it didn't happen that way."

Neither could Nicklaus have expected his favorite haunts would fail to provide him safe harbor. He shot a third-round 81 in a chilling Georgia wind for his worst Masters score in 40 years. A second-round 82 at Pebble Beach was his highest round in 44 U.S. Open starts. He missed a British Open cut at St. Andrews for the first time. They'd turned into the Devil's Triangle. What's more, each of the three, to varying degrees, had undergone some measure of change. It was not that there was anything wrong with them. They were just different—familiar but strange. They were like old friends he did not recognize and who did not remember his name.

"Yeah, they were different," Nicklaus said with a look on his face that seemed far away, or maybe far back in time. "What can I say? The game is changing by the use of strange little things. But the game has always changed. Change is inevitable. It's OK. I have to accept that."

In the same vein, Nicklaus was forced to reconcile himself to the widening gap between his abilities and his aspirations—an irreversible condition. You might say the erosion was not merely physical, but also metaphysical.

"When you're good—I mean really good—you can will that thing into the hole," said Ken Venturi, whose mentors, Ben Hogan and Byron Nelson, possessed a similar aptitude. "Nobody did that more than Jack. He could look at that ball with those eyes and it was like, 'You better go in there you son of a gun, you.' I loved to watch him play golf, because you could see that in him, that ability to have something in his mind and make it happen with the ball."

Nicklaus' career is a highlight reel of clutch putts, starting with the eight-footer for birdie on the 36th hole that secured a 1-up win over Charlie Coe in the 1959 U.S. Amateur at Broadmoor Golf Club in Colorado Springs, Colorado. Then there's the 22-footer (after one of his famous 1-iron shots) to break Hogan's scoring record in the 1967 U.S. Open at Baltusrol; the eight-foot downhill slider that beat Doug Sanders in the 1970 British Open at St. Andrews; the all-but-impossible 40-foot birdie putt at the par-3 16th at Augusta that crushed Weiskopf in 1975; and the 22- and 10-foot birdies to close out the 1980 U.S. Open at Baltusrol. Those are but a few.

But to his chagrin, Nicklaus found time and again that innate ability had disappeared, and with it his economy of strokes. He hadn't lost his nerve, a malady that has stricken many older players. Hogan, at the end, would stand over the ball for interminable lengths until he could summon the fortitude to draw back the putter. Contrarily, Nicklaus just couldn't convert anything; he'd lost his golden touch.

Evidence of autumn.

"I actually feel like I played fairly decent this year, certainly better than I've played in the last four or five years. But I've never putted like this in my life," he said at the British Open. "I've been almost able to will the ball in the hole through most of my life. When I wanted to make a putt I'd figure out how to get it in the hole. And my will is not as strong as it used to be, I guess."

The end result was that Nicklaus fell short in that competition against himself. "I have a standard I set for myself and that's my problem," he said.

You want standards? Some weeks after the U.S. Open, Nicklaus watched a tape of his titanic 3-wood into the 18th green at Pebble Beach, that memorable take-a-bow shot. His reaction? "Horrible swing. It looked like the swing of a guy who is 60 years old instead of a young guy."

Well…

"If I hadn't played well all those years I'd have a lower standard and be happier—probably not, though," he admitted. "I want to play like I've always played. But I can't meet that standard anymore."

Because of that, Nicklaus was prompted to dismiss 2000 as "a terrible year."

But it was hardly a lost year. Not that he ever played for such mundane stakes, but Nicklaus did extend to 43 years his record streak of making the cut in at least one PGA Tour event when he played 72 holes at Augusta National and Muirfield Village. In the latter he was the proud tournament Honoree, and how he ever survived for the weekend amid the tumult is a testament to his well-preserved ability to compartmentalize his mind for a given task.

Far more rewarding, naturally, was his play in the Masters, where once again he let it be known that when he enters the cloistered confines of Augusta National Golf Club he is the embodiment of possibilities. Never mind that he would fade to 54th place, succumbing to the difficult conditions, not to mention the complications age imposes. For two enchanted days Jack Nicklaus threw himself back into his own talent pool, as he hoped he could do, and all of golf eagerly wallowed in the ripples.

"The Masters was the only place where I really did anything," he noted. "It was a good thing because I would have had the grand slam of missed cuts."

But if he hadn't competed, if he hadn't put himself stoutly out there on the line, Nicklaus would have missed the opportunity to bask in the glow of one final display of heartfelt adulation and respect from his many fans—a send-off he rightly deserved and which was diametrically opposite to his reception some 40 years before.

⌒

Jack Nicklaus has been the Olympic flame of golfers.

"There has never been another golfer like him and I doubt there ever will be," Wind said. "I never thought that anyone could be that good for that long. But Jack has always been in a class by himself."

It has not escaped Tiger Woods' attention that Nicklaus set himself apart not only by his performances, but also by his persistence.

"The key to being a great player over a long period of time is consistency," Woods said. "You've got to put yourself into contention week in and week out. You're not going to win every tournament you tee it up in, but you'll get your share of wins. Jack was better than anybody who ever played the game in doing that. For about 15 years there he was in every major championship on the back nine on Sunday. He was in them all."

It wasn't just the majors, either. From 1962-78, a span in which he won a record eight PGA Tour money titles and remained among the top-10 earners, Nicklaus won one of every five events he entered and at least one tournament every year, a 17-year win streak matched only by Arnold Palmer. In his first 25 pro seasons, Nicklaus notched 277 top-10s. Entering the 2000 season, the top tour players on the Official World Rankings, Woods, David Duval, Davis Love III, Ernie Els, and Phil Mickelson, combined had 270 top-10s in 43 seasons.

Now you see what he meant by standards. The mercurial Duval enjoyed one of those brief hot streaks that are common on the PGA Tour when he won 11 times in 34 starts starting at the 1997 Michelob Championship in Williamsburg, Virginia. Greg Norman, Nick Price, Fred Couples, Davis Love III are among those who have gone through similar stages of inspired play.

The trick is sustaining that level of performance, not just for months or years, but decades. That requires a cultivated elixir of confidence, commitment, talent, tenacity, energy, and audacity.

"I think it's taxing to win a lot," Duval said. "It's taxing because you are there every week and if you have a chance to win, whether you win or not, certainly it takes more out of you than if you are teeing off at 9 o'clock Sunday morning—you just don't have the stress levels and the glare of all the people and the media. It takes more out of you when you are playing well."

Which is what Gary Player was talking about when he spoke of Nicklaus' singular brilliance. He was talking about a man who did not shrink in the glare of the spotlight, but instead flourished in that milieu and continually rose to the ineffably difficult challenge associated with seeking victory.

"I put in the context of a great career longevity and Jack is a player who has set a standard in that regard that is so far above the bar," Tom Watson said with obvious reverence. "There was a consistency to him as a player, and as a person, that has been admirable."

True enough. Nicklaus has always colored within the lines. Style, in the form of charisma, often gets confused with substance in the modern age of sports idolatry. But Nicklaus hardly gave a passing thought to image except as it related to excellence of performance and elegance of comportment. In time, this made him easier to appreciate because there was nothing of him to consider but his genius.

↬

Nicklaus never has been much for introspection. Being a good husband and parent is of the utmost importance to him as far as legacies go. "I don't know how to put my career in perspective," he said. "If I've accomplished anything it's as a role model and a standard for upholding the traditions of the game and striving to be the best. The rest of it, that's for others to do."

He cracked open the door a bit more after he was named the greatest male golfer of the twentieth century by the Associated Press. He told the AP's Doug Ferguson: "My legacy might be that I changed an era. I came along during an era where the game was more of a stylish game and I added power. If you look at today's players, they all play with power, so I think I took the game in a different direction."

And everyone was forced to follow him.

One son, Gary, reached the PGA Tour, but in a sense, practically all the golfers of today are sons of Nicklaus. Long before Tiger Woods hung a list of Nicklaus' accomplishments on a wall, the Golden Bear was a yardstick for a generation of players like Watson, Trevino, Weiskopf, Miller, and Crenshaw. He was an inspiration to Greg Norman and John Daly, an idol to Hal Sutton, Ernie Els, and the late Payne Stewart. A teenaged Nick Faldo took up the game after watching Nicklaus on television.

Jack Nicklaus might not have been able to revive his game in 2000, but all he had to do was look around him to see that it was thriving in other players. It is just one facet of his overwhelming impact on golf. The universality of his influence is undeniable. He was a central figure in the formation of today's PGA Tour. His idea to include Europe in the Ryder Cup transformed a sleepy biennial competition into one of the most popular sports events in the world. His sense of dedication and respect for the game spawned one of the most revered and meaningful tournaments in golf, the Memorial. He has been the quintessential professional on and off the golf course, a quality that never waned even as he was forced to confront the inevitable withering of his mighty skills. His style of play had an impact on modern golf course architecture before undertaking a more hands-on role in the design industry. "Jack's style of play was so prodigious," Lanny Wadkins said, "that he changed the shape of the courses we were playing." His competitive record naturally overshadows his career as an architect, but as the number of his works escalates and as he continues to refine his vision, Nicklaus is destined to someday accrue respect as one of the most influential earthmovers.

But always there will be the symbiotic relationship between Nicklaus and the major championships. With forthright intention he made them the central axis of his career. Right or wrong, his single-minded devotion to the majors has become the basis by which we judge the merits of all golfers, past, present, and future.

Two-time major championship winners Johnny Miller and Greg Norman recognize Nicklaus' overwhelming influence on the game's competitive landscape.

"I always tried to treat every tournament the same, but they're not," Miller said. "Obviously, the majors are more important and that's the culture today. That all stems from Jack."

"He really has been the major championships," the two-time British Open Champion Norman said. "He created the major championships to the level they are right now. He approached them in such a way that established them at such a high level."

Because of this, it is difficult to fathom major championship golf without Jack Nicklaus, even though he halted his amazing string in 1998 and missed at least one of each major except the U.S. Open prior to 2000. When hip replacement surgery forced Nicklaus to the Masters sidelines in 1999, Norman was moved to say, "It's like your wife losing the diamond out of the wedding ring."

It was like the extinguishing of the Olympic torch.

"Back when I watched the majors it was to watch Jack and you just naturally expect him always to be there," said Davis Love III. "I don't think we've seen the last of him. But if it's true, it will be different without him. We'll probably feel the same way he did when Byron Nelson and Ben Hogan stopped playing. We'll lose a part of history. He casts a long shadow."

"I hate to see it come to an end," said Hal Sutton, one of the celebrated players labeled the "Next Nicklaus," who as a boy dreamed of beating him in a major and lived that dream at the 1983 PGA at Riviera Country Club when he defeated the Bear by one shot. "I wish it could go on forever."

He's not alone. Fuzzy Zoeller asked rhetorically, "A major without Jack? Are we sure that that's still a major?"

David Gossett, who won the '99 U.S. Amateur at Pebble Beach, 38 years after Nicklaus did it, said the experience of playing with Nicklaus at the Masters and U.S. Open would influence his entire career. Talk about long shadows; Gossett, who happens to be a spot golfer, like Nicklaus, is 40 years younger. "It was not the golf," said Gossett, perceptive as he is precocious. "It was getting a glimpse of the man."

Golf may have defined and illuminated the man, but it is the man and not his golf that is the genuine marvel. Miller, always brash, arrived at this conclusion soon after quizzing Nicklaus' longtime caddie, Angelo Argea. Miller laughs when he recalls how he phrased it. He was blunt, just as he is now.

"You don't really do too much for Jack, do you?" Miller remembers asking Argea. "You don't do yardages, you don't club him, you don't chart the course, don't read the greens. He pays you $1,500 a week, more than anybody else. He must have you doing something. What is it?

"Angelo just looked at me a long time and then said, 'Jack only asks me to do two things. First, when things aren't going good, he wants me to remind him that he's the greatest player in the game. And second, he wants me to remind him that there are still plenty of holes left to play.' Now, if that isn't the essence of the man. That's the ultimate mind-set from one of the ultimate athletes."

Those greatest at their craft—Ali, Aaron, Gretzky, Jordan, and Jack Nicklaus—didn't earn the distinction. They lived it with such fierce intensity that it couldn't help but seep from within them until they not only defeated their rivals, but also redefined the parameters of the very competition in which they took part.

Golf always had been about man against nature until Jack Nicklaus emerged and inserted himself into every golfer's decision matrix. Raymond Floyd said that as golf grew more difficult for everyone else, it became easier for Nicklaus. When Miller shared with Nicklaus his view of the majors, that they were the hardest tournaments to win, Nicklaus corrected him. "You're wrong, they're the easiest to win."

"A light bulb went off in my head," Miller said. "At a regular event everyone's in a comfort zone, but not in the majors. Jack was the kid on the merry-go-round sitting in the middle and just hanging around until everyone else fell off. And he knew they would fall off because he believed in himself and what he was doing."

Which is how he ruled the game for so long—by believing in himself. That's what golf requires. You make a deal with yourself to accept who you are, to trust yourself. Under the supreme pressure of championship golf that's difficult to do, yet Nicklaus made it seem effortless.

There are still plenty of holes left to play.

At the end of his splendid autobiography, *Down the Fairway*, Bobby Jones, just 25 when it was published in 1927, tried to imagine what his life would be like without the crucible of championship golf. He almost seemed to relish the thought. He sounded Darwinian when he wrote:

> "I've been awfully lucky. Maybe I'll win another championship, some day. I love championship competition, after all—win or lose. Sometimes I get to thinking, with a curious little sinking away down deep, how I will feel when my tournament days are over, and I read in the papers that the boys are gathering for the national open, or the amateur…Maybe at one of the courses I love so well, and where I fought in the old days…It's going to be queer.
>
> "But there's always one thing to look forward to—the round with Dad and Chick and Brad; the Sunday morning round at old East Lake, with nothing to worry about, when championships are done."

Nicklaus has a similar appreciation for that crucible, the majors. Eerily, some of his words in the latter part of the year conveyed sentiments similar to Jones. Charlie Nicklaus would have liked the comparison.

"A lot of great things have happened to me in my life," Nicklaus said. "It just so happens, though, when you're playing golf and you're playing tournament golf there aren't many things better."

And there was this thought, too, just before the PGA: "I suppose… I guess…it's time for me to let go. And once I let go of all the other tournaments—the ones I let go this year—then I might enjoy some leisurely golf where it's not important, because I don't have anything to play for or prepare for and it will be fine…But I don't know when."

So it goes. You can be sure that when the boys are gathering at future Masters, PGA Championships or national opens, Nicklaus will feel that curious sinking away down deep. But unlike Jones, one suspects Nicklaus will not relish such times, when championships are done.

Someone put the question to him at Valhalla. Would he like to be 30 years younger? "I always wish I was 30 years younger (but) I'm quite happy where I am. I've had a great career. I wouldn't want to spend the next 20 years trying to beat him (Woods)." He took a breath, caught himself and reversed field. "Yeah, I would. Of course I would. I've always liked a challenge."

There he was, the same old Nicklaus, unwilling to give an inch or concede a thing. Wouldn't that have been something to see, the two titans in their prime locked in epic battles? You know that Nicklaus would have thrived, win or lose, in that setting. He has always savored challenges. But there is more to it than that, something deeper, primordial. Life is full of challenges. Golf is the one challenge that is his life.

"I love the game; it has meant so much to me, and to my life," he conceded. "I like the competition. I love to compete. That's who I am."

And because that's who he is, for Jack Nicklaus there never will be a time when championships are done. Not in his mind, not in ours. That's who we know—the champion golfer who defied nature and locked himself in his own springtime.

Dawn or twilight?

In 2000, we watched Jack Nicklaus at twilight. But we'll always remember him at dawn, that element of time when possibilities seem endless, when the sun rises to greet the man who only looks ahead to his own destiny.

When there are always plenty of holes left to play.

APPENDIX

In the beginning I mentioned golf's convenient conversion to words. Stories of the game can be told handsomely with numbers as well, and it will be a long time before any golfer approaches the astounding numbers compiled by Jack Nicklaus.

The benchmark figure in golf is 18 major professional championships. That was the result of decades of pursuit. However, there exist so many more revealing statistics—statistics compiled along the way to those victories—that present a broader and richer tale of the Golden Bear's 159 performances in golf's Grand Slam tournaments through 2000.

My associate, Alex Miceli, who loves the unflinching realism of numbers, pulled together a collection of fascinating and, in some cases, esoteric facts and figures of cardinal and ordinal value. It's our way of coloring in just a little more of the background and adding another coat of varnish to the incandescent Nicklaus standard.

Jack Nicklaus in the Majors

Jack Nicklaus began playing major championships as a professional at the 1962 Masters against the likes of Ben Hogan, Arnold Palmer, Gary Player, Gene Littler, Jimmy Demaret, and Billy Casper. He would finish tied for 15th at that Masters, but would make an immediate and telling improvement in major competition two months later at Oakmont Country Club in Oakmont, Pennsylvania, in the backyard of the "King," Palmer. Nicklaus would win his first major, defeating Palmer in a play-off, and thus began a run unequaled in the annals of championship golf.

While Nicklaus has competed well in the majors right up to his sixth-place finish in the 1998 Masters, he enjoyed one distinct 20-year period of dominance. From 1962 through the '82 season, Nicklaus competed in 84 majors; he finished out of the Top 25 only eight times, or 0.095 percent. During that same period he won 17 majors, 20.2 percent of the majors he entered. He won at least one major in 13 different years, and in five different years he recorded two victories.

In his career, both amateur and professional, Nicklaus has had 21 years in which he had multiple top-10 finishes. He also recorded multiple top-5 finishes 16 of those 21 years. He is, indeed, the enduring standard.

Majors won by Jack Nicklaus

1962 U.S. Open at Oakmont Country Club, in a play-off over Arnold Palmer

1963 Masters at Augusta National Golf Club, over Tony Lema by 1 stroke

1963 PGA Championship at the Dallas Athletic Club, over Dave Ragan by 2 strokes

1965 Masters at Augusta National Golf Club, over Arnold Palmer and Gary Player by 9 strokes

1966 Masters at Augusta National Golf Club, in a play-off over Tommy Jacobs and Gay Brewer

1966 British Open at Muirfield, over Doug Sanders and Dave Thomas by 1 stroke

1967 U.S. Open at Baltusrol Golf Club, over Arnold Palmer by 4 strokes

1970 British Open at St. Andrews, in a play-off over Doug Sanders

1971 PGA Championship at PGA National Golf Club, over Billy Casper by 2 strokes

1972 Masters at Augusta National Golf Club, over Bruce Crampton, Bobby Mitchell, and Tom Weiskopf by 3 strokes

1972 U.S. Open at Pebble Beach Golf Links, over Bruce Crampton by 3 strokes

1973 PGA Championship at Canterbury Golf Club, over Bruce Crampton by 4 strokes

1975 Masters at Augusta National Golf Club, over Johnny Miller and Tom Weiskopf by 1 stroke

1975 PGA Championship at Firestone Country Club, over Bruce Crampton by 2 strokes

1978 British Open at St. Andrews over Ben Crenshaw, Ray Floyd, Tom Kite and Simon Owen by 2 strokes

1980 U.S. Open at Baltusrol Golf Club, over Isao Aoki by 2 strokes

1980 PGA Championship at Oak Hill Country Club, over Andy Bean by 7 strokes

1986 Masters at Augusta National Golf Club, over Tom Kite and Greg Norman by 1 stroke

Nicklaus' Record in the Majors, 1962-82

Wins	Seconds	Top 5s	Top 10s	Top 25s
17 (20.23%)	16 (19.05%)	51 (60.71%)	63 (75.00%)	76 (90.48%)

Years with Multiple Top 10s in Majors

'61 (2)[a]	'66 (3)*	'73 (4)*	'79 (3)*
'62 (2)	'67 (3)*	'74 (4)*	'80 (3)*
'63 (3)*	'68 (3)*	'75 (4)*	'81 (3)*
'64 (3)*	'70 (3)	'76 (3)*	'82 (2)
'65 (2)*	'71 (4)*	'77 (4)*	
	'72 (3)*	'78 (3)	

*(a) Denotes Amateur   * Denotes multiple top 5s in that year*

Nicklaus' Record at the Masters

Year	1st	2nd	3rd	Final	Score	Position
2000	74	70	81	78	303	T-54
1998	73	72	70	68	283	T-6
1997	77	70	74	78	299	T-39
1996	70	73	76	78	297	T-41
1995	67	78	70	75	290	T-35
1994	78	74			152	Cut
1993	67	75	76	71	289	T-27
1992	69	75	69	74	287	T-42
1991	68	72	72	76	288	T-35
1990	72	70	69	74	285	6
1989	73	74	73	71	291	T-18
1988	75	73	72	72	292	T-21
1987	74	72	73	70	289	T-7
1986	**74**	**71**	**69**	**65**	**279**	**Win**
1985	71	74	72	69	286	T-6
1984	73	73	70	70	286	T-18
1983	73				73	WD
1982	69	77	71	75	292	T-15
1981	70	65	75	72	282	T-2
1980	74	71	73	73	291	T-33
1979	69	71	72	69	281	4
1978	73	72	69	67	281	7
1977	72	70	70	66	278	2
1976	67	69	73	73	282	T-3

Year	1st	2nd	3rd	Final	Score	Position
1975	**68**	**67**	**73**	**68**	**276**	**Win**
1974	69	71	72	69	281	T-4
1973	69	77	73	66	285	T-3
1972	**68**	**71**	**73**	**74**	**286**	**Win**
1971	70	71	68	72	281	T-2
1970	71	75	69	69	284	8
1969	68	75	72	76	291	T-24
1968	69	71	74	67	281	T-5
1967	72	79			151	Cut
1966	**68**	**76**	**72**	**72**	**288**	**Win**
1965	**67**	**71**	**64**	**69**	**271**	**Win**
1964	71	73	71	67	282	T-2
1963	**74**	**66**	**74**	**72**	**286**	**Win**
1962	74	75	70	72	291	T-15
1961(a)	70	75	70	72	287	T-7
1960(a)	75	71	72	75	293	T-13
1959(a)	76	74			150	Cut

Wins: 6

Runner-Up: 4

Lowest Masters score: 64

Highest Masters score: 81

Number of appearances: 41 (38 professional, 3 amateur)

Number of holes: 2,736*

Includes 18 holes from play-off in 1966

First round scoring average: 71.05

Second round scoring average: 72.43

Third round scoring average: 73.94

Final round scoring average: 73.44

Scoring average: 72.66

Wins	Seconds	Top 5s	Top 10s	Top 25s
6 (15.79%)	4 (10.53%)	15 (39.47%)	22 (57.89%)	28 (73.68%)

Nicklaus in his prime at the Masters (1963-79):

- Jack Nicklaus played in 18 Masters. He missed one cut and won 5 times.
- Excluding the year he missed the cut, Nicklaus averaged a 4th place finish in the other 17 appearances.
- Key to his run: first round performance. He averaged sixth with a scoring average of 69.71 after the first round.
- Scoring average: 70.68
- Rounds under par: 39
- Rounds in the 60s: 27
- Rounds at par: 9
- Rounds over par: 18

Notable Masters records held or shared:

- Most victories: 6
- Most runner-up finishes: 4
- Oldest winner: 46 years, 2 months, 23 days (1986)
- Oldest top-10 finisher: 58 years, 2 months, 21 days (tied 6th, 1998)
- Oldest player with low 72 holes: 283 (1998)
- Most subpar 72-hole scores: 22
- Most par or better 72-hole scores: 24
- Most subpar rounds: 71
- Most consecutive subpar rounds: 7
- Most rounds par or better: 93
- Most sub-70 rounds: 39
- Most top-3 finishes: 12
- Most top-5 finishes: 15
- Most top-10 finishes: 22
- Most top-25 finishes: 29
- Most 72-hole finishes: 36
- Most final rounds par or better: 24

Nicklaus' Record at the U.S. Open

Year	1st	2nd	3rd	Final	Score	Position
2000	73	82			155	Cut
1999	78	75			153	Cut
1998	73	74	73	75	295	T-43
1997	73	71	75	74	293	T-52
1996	72	74	69	72	287	T-27
1995	71	81			152	Cut
1994	69	70	77	76	292	T-28
1993	70	72	76	71	289	T-72
1992	77	74			151	Cut
1991	70	76	77	74	297	T-46
1990	71	74	68	76	289	T-33
1989	67	74	74	75	290	T-43
1988	74	73			147	Cut
1987	70	68	76	77	291	T-46
1986	77	72	67	68	284	T-8
1985	76	73			149	Cut
1984	71	71	70	77	289	T-21
1983	73	74	77	76	300	T-43
1982	74	70	71	69	284	2
1981	69	68	71	72	280	T-6
1980	**63**	**71**	**70**	**68**	**272**	**Win**
1979	74	77	72	68	291	T-9
1978	73	69	74	73	289	T-6
1977	74	68	71	72	285	T-10
1976	74	70	75	68	287	T-11
1975	72	70	75	72	289	T-7
1974	75	74	76	69	294	T-10
1973	71	69	74	68	282	T-4
1972	**71**	**73**	**72**	**74**	**290**	**Win**
1971	69	72	68	71	280	2
1970	81	72	75	76	304	T-51
1969	74	67	75	73	289	T-25
1968	72	70	70	67	279	2

Year	1st	2nd	3rd	Final	Score	Position
1967	**71**	**67**	**72**	**65**	**275**	**Win**
1966	71	71	69	74	285	3
1965	78	72	73	76	299	T-32
1964	72	73	77	73	295	T-23
1963	76	77			153	Cut
1962	**72**	**70**	**72**	**69**	**283**	**Win**
1961(a)	75	69	70	70	284	T-4
1960(a)	71	71	69	71	282	2
1959(a)	77	77			154	Cut
1958(a)	79	75	73	77	304	T-41
1957(a)	80	80			160	Cut

Wins: 4

Runner-Up: 4

Lowest U.S. Open score: 63

Highest U.S. Open score: 82

Number of Appearances: 44 (39 professional, 5 amateur)

Number of holes: 2,592*

First round scoring average: 72.59

Second round scoring average: 72.26

Third round scoring average: 72.84

Final round scoring average: 72.13

Scoring average: 72.45

* *Includes 18 holes for 1972 play-off and 18 holes for 1962 play-off*

Wins	Seconds	Top 5s	Top 10s	Top 25s
4 (9.09%)	4 (9.09%)	9 (20.45%)	16 (36.36%)	18 (40.90%)

Nicklaus at his best in the U.S. Open (1971-82):

- Nicklaus played in 12 U.S. Opens, never missing a cut and winning twice while not finishing worse than a tie for 11th.
- He finished in the top 10 in 11 of 12 years.
- Key to his run: final round scoring. During that period he averaged sixth place, with a scoring average of 70.33 in his final round.
- Scoring average: 71.31
- Rounds under par: 18
- Rounds in the 60s: 14
- Rounds at par: 4
- Rounds over par: 26

Notable U.S. Open records held or shared

Most victories: 4

Most runner-up finishes: 4

Most top-5 finishes: 11

Most top-10 finishes: 18

Most top-25 finishes: 22

Lowest aggregate 72-hole score: 272

Lowest 18-hole score: 63

Lowest first 36 holes: 134

Most consecutive Open starts: 44

Most 72-hole finishes: 35

Most subpar rounds: 35

Most subpar 72-hole totals: 7

Most sub-70 scores: 29

Longest span, first to last win: 18 years

Nicklaus' Record at Selected U.S. Open Courses

Course	Rounds	Ave. Score	Par	Best Finish	Worst Finish
Baltusrol Golf Club	12	69.66	70	Win (1967, 80)	T-72 (1993)
Cherry Hills Country Club	8	71.38	71	2 (1960)	T-6 (1978)
Congressional Country Club	8	73.75	70	T-23 (1964)	T-52 (1997)
Hazeltine National Golf Club	8	75.13	72	T-46 (1991)	T-51 (1970)
Inverness Club	6	75.16	70/71	T-9 (1979)	Cut (1957)
Medinah Country Club	8	72.25	71/72	T-7 (1975)	T-33 (1990)
Merion Golf Club	8	70.0	70	2 (1971)	T-6 (1981)
Oak Hill Country Club	8	71.13	70	2 (1968)	T-43 (1989)
Oakland Hills Country Club	6	72.67	70	T-27 (1996)	Cut (1985)
Oakmont Country Club	16	72.31	72/71	Win (1962)	T-43 (1983)
Olympic Golf Club	12	72.58	70	3 (1966)	T-46 (1987)
Pebble Beach Golf Links	12	73.33	72/71	Win (1972)	Cut (1992, 00)
Shinnecock Hills Golf Club	6	72.66	70	T-8 (1986)	Cut (1995)
Southern Hills Country Club	8	73.63	70	T-10 (1977)	T-41 (1958)
The Country Club	4	75.0	71		Cut (1963, 88)
Winged Foot Golf Club	8	72.88	70	T-10 (1974)	T-21 (1984)

Nicklaus' Record at the British Open

Year	1st	2nd	3rd	Final	Score	Position
2000	77	73			150	Cut
1997	73	74	71	75	293	T-60
1996	69	66	77	73	285	T-44
1995	78	70	77	71	296	T-79
1994	72	73			145	Cut
1993	69	75			144	Cut
1992	75	73			148	Cut
1991	70	75	69	71	285	T-44
1990	71	70	77	71	289	T-63
1989	74	71	71	70	286	T-30
1988	75	70	75	68	288	T-25
1987	74	71	81	76	302	T-72
1986	78	73	76	71	298	T-46
1985	77	75			152	Cut
1984	76	72	68	72	288	T-31
1983	71	72	72	70	285	T-29
1982	77	70	72	69	288	T-10
1981	83	66	71	70	290	T-23
1980	73	67	71	69	280	T-4
1979	72	69	73	72	286	T-2
1978	**71**	**72**	**69**	**69**	**281**	**Win**
1977	68	70	65	66	269	2
1976	74	70	72	69	285	T-2
1975	69	71	68	72	280	T-3
1974	74	72	70	71	287	3
1973	69	70	76	65	280	4
1972	70	72	71	66	279	2
1971	71	71	72	69	283	T-5
1970	**68**	**69**	**73**	**73**	**283**	**Win**
1969	75	70	68	72	285	T-6
1968	76	69	73	73	291	T-2
1967	71	69	71	69	280	2
1966	**70**	**67**	**75**	**70**	**282**	**Win**
1965	73	71	77	73	294	T-12
1964	76	74	66	68	284	2
1963	71	67	70	70	278	3
1962	80	72	74	79	305	T-34

Wins: 3

Runner-Up: 7

Lowest British Open score: 65

Highest British Open score: 83

Number of appearances: 37

Number of holes: 2,522*

Includes 18 holes for 1970 play-off

First round scoring average: 73.24

Second round scoring average: 70.84

Third round scoring average: 72.22

Final round scoring average: 70.69

Scoring average: 71.77

Wins	Seconds	Top 5s	Top 10s	Top 25s
3 (8.10%)	7 (18.92%)	16 (43.24%)	18 (48.65%)	21 (56.76%)

Nicklaus in his prime at the British Open (1963-80):

- From 1963 to 1980, he played in 18 British Opens with his worst finish a tie for 12th at Royal Lytham in 1969. It was his only finish out of the top 6.
- Key to his run: final round scoring. Nicklaus averaged third place, with a scoring average of 69.77.
- During that 18 years he had 7 seconds, 3 thirds, 2 fourths, 1 fifth, and 1 sixth.
- Scoring average: 70.65
- Rounds under par: 40
- Rounds in the 60s: 25
- Rounds at par: 10
- Rounds over par: 22

Notable British Open records held or shared:

- Most runner-up finishes: 7
- Lowest aggregate score by runner-up: 269 (1977)
- Most top-3 finishes: 13
- Most top-5 finishes: 16
- Most top-10 finishes: 18
- Most top-25 finishes: 21
- Most rounds under 70: 33
- Most 72-hole finishes: 32

Nicklaus' Record at Selected British Open Courses

Course	Rounds	Ave. Score	Par	Best Finish	Worst Finish
Carnoustie	8	71.38	72	T-2 (1968)	T-3 (1975)
Muirfield	18	71.72	71	Win (1966)	Cut (1992)
Royal Birkdale	20	71.60	73/72/71/70	T-2 (1976)	T-44 (1991)
Royal Lytham	24	71.20	71	T-2 (1979)	T-44 (1996)
Royal St. George's	8	73.25	70	T-23 (1981)	Cut (1985, 93)
St. Andrews	26	71.96	72	Win (1970, 78)	Cut (2000)
Royal Troon	20	72.75	72/71	4th (1973)	T-60 (1997)
Turnberry	10	71.20	70	2 (1977)	Cut (1994)

Nicklaus' Record at the PGA Championship

Year	1st	2nd	3rd	Final	Score	Position
2000	77	71			148	Cut
1997	74	76			150	Cut
1996	77	69			146	Cut
1995	69	71	71	76	287	T-67
1994	79	71			150	Cut
1993	71	73			144	Cut
1992	72	78			150	Cut
1991	71	72	73	71	287	T-23
1990	78	74			152	Cut
1989	68	72	73	72	285	T-27
1988	72	79			151	Cut
1987	76	73	74	73	296	T-24
1986	70	68	72	75	285	T-16
1985	66	75	74	74	289	T-32
1984	77	70	71	69	287	T-25
1983	73	65	71	66	275	2
1982	74	70	72	67	283	T-16
1981	71	68	71	69	279	T-4
1980	**70**	**69**	**66**	**69**	**274**	**Win**
1979	73	72	78	71	294	T-65
1978	79	74			153	Cut
1977	69	71	70	73	283	3
1976	71	69	69	74	283	T-4
1975	**70**	**68**	**67**	**71**	**276**	**Win**
1974	69	69	70	69	277	2
1973	**72**	**68**	**68**	**69**	**277**	**Win**
1972	72	75	68	72	287	T-13
1971	**69**	**69**	**70**	**73**	**281**	**Win**
1970	68	76	73	66	283	T-6
1969	70	68	74	71	283	T-11
1968	71	79			150	Cut
1967	67	75	69	71	282	T-3
1966	75	71	75	71	292	T-22

Year	1st	2nd	3rd	Final	Score	Position
1965	69	70	72	71	282	T-2
1964	67	73	70	64	274	T-2
1963	**69**	**73**	**69**	**68**	**279**	**Win**
1962	71	74	69	67	281	T-3

Wins: 5

Runner-Up: 4

Lowest PGA Championship score: 64

Highest PGA Championship score: 79

Number of Appearances: 37

Number of Holes: 2,304

First round scoring average: 71.86

Second round scoring average: 71.84

Third round scoring average: 71.07

Final round scoring average: 70.44

Scoring average: 71.38

Wins	Seconds	Top 5s	Top 10s	Top 25s
5 (13.51%)	4 (10.81%)	14 (37.84%)	15 (40.54%)	23 (62.16%)

Nicklaus in his prime at the PGA Championship (1962-77):

- From 1962 to 1977, Nicklaus played in 16 PGA Championships, with one cut missed, in 1968.
- He finished out of the top 10 only three times and finished in the top 5 11 times.
- Key to his run: final round scoring. During that period he averaged fourth place in 15 of the 16 years with a scoring average of 70.00;
- In that 16-year stretch, Nicklaus had 3 seconds, 3 thirds, 1 fourth, and 1 sixth.
- Scoring average: 70.48
- Rounds under par: 33
- Rounds in the 60s: 27
- Rounds at par: 5
- Rounds over par: 24

Notable PGA Championship records held or shared:

- Most victories: 5
- Most runner-up finishes: 4
- Largest winning margin: 7 strokes (1980)
- Most appearances: 37
- Most rounds played: 128
- Most top-3 finishes: 12
- Most top-5 finishes: 14
- Most top-10 finishes: 15
- Most top-25 finishes: 23
- Most subpar rounds: 53
- Most sub-70 rounds: 41
- Most cuts made: 27

Nicklaus' Record at Selected PGA Championship Courses

Course	Rounds	Ave. Score	Par	Best Finish	Worst Finish
Canterbury Golf Club	4	69.25	71	Win (1973)	
Dallas Athletic Club	4	69.75	71	Win (1963)	
Firestone Country Club	8	71.0	70	Win (1975)	T-22 (1966)
Inverness Club	6	71.5	71	T-16 (1986)	Cut (1993)
Oak Hill Country Club	8	70.13	70	Win (1980)	T-13 (1972)
Oakland Hills Country Club	8	72.63	70	T-13 (1972)	T-64 (1979)
PGA National Golf Club	8	72.13	72	Win (1971)	T-24 (1987)
Riviera Country Club	8	70.25	71	2 (1983)	T-67 (1995)
Shoal Creek Club	6	73.17	72	T-25 (1984)	Cut (1990)
Southern Hills Country Club	10	71.60	70	T-6 (1970)	Cut (1994)
Valhalla Golf Club	4	73.50	72		Cut (1996, 2000)

ACKNOWLEDGMENTS

Writing a book, while a lonely endeavor, is never completed alone. I know I wasn't alone.

Along the way you draw friends, colleagues, family, officials and even innocent bystanders into this vortex, a virtual universe of your own making that bears no resemblance to real life, which isn't all bad.

In any event, here are the people to whom I owe a great deal of gratitude—or apologies, depending on the perspective.

Let's start at the top. This book could not have been completed without the immense generosity and patience of Jack and Barbara Nicklaus. They have my deepest thanks. They were patient, they were helpful, they went above and beyond in indulging my curiosity about matters great and small. Obviously, the year was an important one for them, yet, the amount of time they sacrificed on my behalf and the genuine goodwill with which they did it are gestures I will never forget. Likewise, I must thank the Nicklaus children—Jackie, Steve, Nan, Gary and Michael—and their families for being so wonderfully delightful and never making me feel like I was butting in, even when I was.

Others to thank, and there are many:

Scott Tolley, director of communications for Golden Bear International, for his efforts to fill in the multitude of blanks common to any such huge project, but more for his unwavering positive outlook and his genuine friendship. Scott Lubin, who caddied for Jack and carries himself with poise and integrity; there are few people as friendly and as unassuming, just a joy to know and to hang out with in your local Ale House or other fine beverage establishment, if only to watch the women drool over him. Also thanks to Ron Hurst—trusted pilot, down-to-earth person.

Thanks to PGA Tour commissioner Tim Finchem. To Bob Combs for his support and wisdom, and to the Tour staff, including: Dave Lancer, Jeff Adams, Lee Patterson, Helen Ross, Joan von Thron Alexander, Phil Stambaugh, Dave Senko, James Cramer, Denise Taylor, Nelson Luis, Ana Leaird, Chris Smith, Toni Billie, and Ward Clayton.

To Craig Smith, Pete Kowalski, Suzanne Colson, and Rand Jerris from the U.S. Golf Association. At the PGA of America, the always-resplendent Julius Mason, Jamie Roggero, and Bob Denney. Also, to Stuart McDougal of the Royal and Ancient. And to Glenn Greenspan at Augusta National Golf Club, a man whose job pressures never cease and whose disposition seldom strays from sunny.

To the good folks at Muirfield Village Golf Club: John Hines, Dan Sullivan, John Stelzer, Mike McBride, Ivor and Carol Young, Bob and Louise Hoag, Pandel Savic, and the Wisler clan. Ken and Jean Bowden, also take a bow.

A huge thank-you to Alex Miceli for making it all possible and for not killing me in Scotland. I'll always remember our ride in the milk truck into St. Andrews. And another to Stuart Hall for his sobering perspective.

To colleagues and friends for their varied and valuable contributions throughout the year: Doug Ferguson, Ken Carpenter, Denny Schreiner, Tony Nelson, Rob Oller, Steve Ellis, Tom Stine, Dick Mudry, Brian Hewitt, Jeff Babineau, Cliff Brown, Len Shapiro, Jeff Rude, Jim Nugent, Bob Baptist, Tim Rosaforte, Frank Antonelli, Mike Hurdzan, Bob Bubka, Janis Self, Rusty Miller, Linn Nishikawa, Gary Planos, Marty Keiter, Bruce Hooley, John Garrity, Craig Dolch, John Hawkins, Gary Van Sickle, Jaime Diaz, T.R. Reinman, Alister Nicol, Hunki Yun, Thomas Bonk, Alan Shipnuck, Randy Mell, Doc Giffin, Andy O'Brien, Gary Taylor, John Holmes, Kaye Kessler, Dan O'Neill, Marino Parascenzo, Jim Nantz, Mark Rolfing, Gary McCord, Johnny Miller, Roger Maltbie, Gary Koch, Ken Venturi, Dan Hicks, Mike Tirico, Jimmy Roberts, Jerry Pate, R.J. Harper, Diane Stracuzzi, Cathy Scherzer, Peter Kessler, Robin Brendle, Leslie Ann Wade, Tommy Roy, Jack Graham, Lance Barrow, Tommy Spencer, Burch Riber, Larry Lambrecht, Marc Feldman, Kip Erickson, Larry Hasek, Don Wade, Bill Paul, Melanie Hauser, Steve Brener, Toby Zwikel, Judi Janofsky, Ray Hustek, Doug Sobieski, and the indefatigable Art Spander.

To Brian Lewis, Karmel Bycraft (the can-do lady), Brett Marshall, Lynne Johnson, Danny Freels, and all the terrific folks at Sleeping Bear Press.

Lastly, but most importantly, thanks to my family: Denise, Alexander, and Elizabeth. They made tremendous sacrifices during a year in which I was home too infrequently and was working too feverishly to be able give them the time I wanted to or that which they deserved.

Alex and Ellie are my two most prized possessions. Alex, 5 years old, actually helped with the writing chore. Or at least he believed he was doing so. I was stricken with the flu in mid-October and bedridden for two days, missing the Presidents Cup. The first morning Alex decided to sit at my desk, turned on my computer and began punching the keyboard. Asked by my wife what he was doing, Alex, who usually plays video games ("Pajama Sam" is his favorite), said in all earnestness, "I'm working for daddy today." No royalty could top that.

My three-year-old daughter, Ellie, meanwhile, provided the kind of consistent interruptions that might have been otherwise unwelcome were she not the most adorable human being on the planet. This book was written during one of a parent's most coveted periods—when their children actually want them around. My daughter happened to be particularly insistent of my involvement in the details of her life, from fetching her chocolate milk, to bathing her, combing her hair and singing lullabies. Is "The Pooh Song" supposed to make us cry?

Then there is my wife, Denise. Aside from love, patience, and support, Denise injected the proper proportions of understanding and levity while I suffered through the inevitable ebbs and flows of the writing process. Especially memorable was her dubious reaction during a particularly arid stretch when I announced four nights in a row that I was "almost done with Chapter 6." The look on her face was priceless.

Of course, I have to mention more family, because they are the elements that make up the sum of who I am, because I love them, and because the list is short and won't take a lot of space: Dad, Mom (for reasons too numerous), Grandma Shed, Mindy, Chet, Cindy, Alison, Sarah and Steve, Elaine and (Uncle) Jerry, Julieanne, Nicky; also Ed and Jo, Eddie (or Skippy?), Nanny Monkey, Tom and Jean, Shawn, Matthew, Amy, Paul and Connie.

A special tribute to those who have gone before, who worked hard, lived simply, made sacrifices for their family and blazed the trail: Mary, Linus, and Chester. Their spirits live. They can go wherever they want.

There, that should cover it.

Told you I wasn't alone.